Jonisha Rios

Curse of
The
Blue Vagina

& other stories

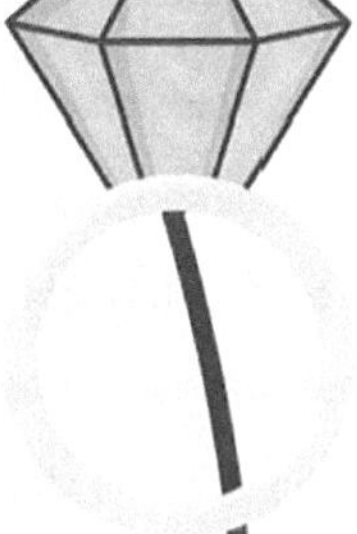

Copyright 2015 Jonisha Rios

All rights reserved. No portion of this publication may be reproduced or utilized in any form or by any means, electronic or mechanical, including photocopying, without permission in writing from the publisher. In all cases, the editors and writers have made efforts to ensure that the credits are given to appropriate people and organizations. If any infringement has been made, the publisher will be glad, upon receiving notification, to make appropriate acknowledgement in future editions of the book. Inquiries should be addressed to Jonisha Rios blameitonrios@gmail.com. Or visit Savedbythepole.com, or blameitonrioslive.com.

13 ISBN: 978-1-63393-014-8

Editing: Elizabeth Lopez

Cover Design: Tim Pryor of Pryority Design Studio,

www.pryoritydesignstudio.com

Cartoon Illustration: Ed Mouzon

Design & Layout: Debbi Stocco,

mybookdesigner.com

Printed in the USA

Published by

Café con Leche

Dedication

To my son Iysaac-Brendon; You bring me such joy! Thank you for teaching me how to love again. To the man that helped create him, Pookie you are the man of my dreams...now let's have sex.

Awkward transition but to my parents, thanks for having sex and making me—I love you both.

To my sister, close friends and women everywhere:

Always remember we are like the sea in the middle of its storm, passionate, fierce, and on a calm day warm and inviting—therefore embrace your emotions, it means we are alive.

Finally, to my hamster Fiesty Rodriguez...you had me at "squeak squeak."

Table of Contents

Note from the Author	vi
CURSE OF THE BLUE VAGINA	7
Epilogue	104
NUDE IN NEW YORK	107
Epilogue	189
EXPOSED	193
Acknowledgements	252
About the Author	257

Note from the Author

Because we are currently in the midst of workshopping and producing these shows regularly, the stories are currently a reflection of where we are right now in the process. In other words if you see the show and it becomes something totally different from what you read in the book, just go with it. That's the process.

CURSE OF THE
BLUE VAGINA

I bet you're wondering why I'm sitting in a cramped jail cell wearing my wedding dress the morning of my Big Day. Well, I sorta lost it at breakfast. Only I would never actually hurt anyone. Besides I'm Latina. I'm a good person by nature. Contrary to what most people think, we aren't all hot-tempered, that is, unless you did something to seriously piss us off. What were they thinking locking me up like this? I mean if the people at the IHOP thought I could kill anyone with a spork, then they're crazier than I am. A spork wouldn't even pierce the skin. Trust me I know. My sister tried stabbing me with one after I ate the last chocolate Jell-O-pudding pop when we were kids.

In exactly two hours and forty-five minutes, I'm scheduled to become *Mrs.* Ray Lopez. The title of Mrs. is a big deal in my Nuyorican family because it means that not only would I escape life as an old maid, but also that the rumors of me being gay would finally be laid to rest. I'm set to get married at a low-key chapel called Saint Luke's. It's the only church in town that typically takes in more funeral services than weddings. Sure, Uncle Paco and a string of other dead relatives had been carried down that aisle before me. Who cares? I'm determined to make my "Special Day" happen come hell or come high water. Besides, the church was in need of some money so I booked it for a steal of a deal.

I'm running out of time and the officer out there refused to let me make my one phone call, until I "calm down," so everyone at the church will probably think I went AWOL. Oh well, fuck it, at least now I get to have some time to be by myself and get to the bottom of my meltdown.

My relationship with Ray has never been smooth or easy. In fact, lately it seems like we've been apart longer than we've been together. Thing is, despite that, I thought we had our shit together and were moving ahead. Now I may never get married, and it's all because of *the Curse of the Blue Vagina*!

"What is that?" you ask. To put it simply *the Curse of the Blue Vagina* is to women what *Blue Balls* are to men. Problem is when men get "Blue Balls", they are left physically unsatisfied, which is temporary, and when women get the "Blue Vagina", they are left emotionally unsatisfied, which lasts forever. You may think that this *Curse* is total nonsense, but it's not, it's very real it causes your vag to turn a bluish-tinted color that creates a recurring painful sensation that ultimately leads to heartbreak. And it is not to be confused with *Bacterial Vaginosis* or *the Blue Waffle Disease* that creates a similar blue discoloration. No! This kind of BV comes with its own different set of symptoms along with a plethora of blue shades to match that ultimately take an emotional toll on you. To make matters worse, it only seems to affect a certain portion of the Latina population. (Mostly those of us who were raised in conservative Catholic families, where guilt is part of our natural upbringing.)

It is said when you have BV, not even El Cuco himself will come and haunt you. You become like a walking stick of dynamite. Don't even think about making yourself all cozy on Abuelitas plastic covered couch because you're likely to burn a hole right through it.

This is not some old wives' tale either. There's a documented history of women out there who have devastating stories to tell. If you don't believe me, just go to your local Santera, and she'll pull out a dusty old book, something as fearsome and heavy as the Bible. In there is where all our sisters have gone astray. If you don't pay attention to how you're living your life, it will strike you down like the plague.

It's horrible. Your mind gets all fuzzy and your heart starts palpitating. Your stomach feels like you have butterflies fluttering then dive-bombing to their death. This ain't nerves. Your body gets rocked by convulsions like it's expelling the very devil himself.

And here is the kicker—apparently I'm stuck with this unless I find out what caused it, and break the spell once and for all. *The Curse* came back to haunt me last night at my bachelorette party.

*S*urprise!" Everyone shouted as I entered my sister Mariana's studio apartment. Her place is so small you could use the toilet and bake cookies in the same room. I grabbed a glass of wine off the coffee table. As I cocked my head back to chug it down, I noticed a larger-than-life pink penis piñata hanging from the ceiling.

"Nice penis," I said to Marianna sarcastically as I made myself comfortable on the foldout IKEA futon. How she expected us to swing a bat at this candy-filled penis in this small ass room, blindfolded, was beyond me. The room was decorated with every penis accessory you could imagine: penis balloons, penis-shaped lollipops and everyone was donning an erect towering penis party hat. I sat there like a big pus just taking it all in.

I guess none of my friends got the invite because as I scanned the room, the only people I recognized aside from my mom, grandma, and sister, were my lesbian aunt Luisa and her roommate Ming.

My mother approached me holding two wine glasses. She has a unique medical condition. It's a combination obsessive-compulsive disorder and Tourette's—in Spanish it's called loca. "It's time for the toast!" she exclaimed as she raised her glass. "To my daughter..." she trailed off as she started inspecting the glass.

"Wait a second," she paused. "DIOS MIO!" she shouted in Spanish. "There is a spot on the glass." She brought it close to her face. "Right here!"

Before she could mumble obscenities under her breath, Marianna darted into the kitchen area, grabbed a sponge and handed it to her then pulled her glass away and continued the toast.

"To my sister, for finding such a good guy, we wish you the very best. Cheers!" Marianna proclaimed, trying to diffuse the smudged glass situation. The women held up their glasses and took a sip.

They all looked so happy, but I wasn't. Everyone assumed my fiancé Ray was great because he was a sweet Latino with a job. But, he wasn't what I would call perfect.

"So how did you meet Mr. Wonderful?" Ming asked innocently, as she sipped her wine from a penis-shaped straw.

Everyone in the room grew silent anxiously anticipating the story of our meeting. I smiled graciously, took another swig from my glass and began sharing my fairytale version of the story.

"Um, actually, Ray and I met at a Borders' Going out of Business sale," I looked at my ring to avoid eye contact. "We were both reaching for the last copy of *How to Meet Your Other Half*." Everyone gasped, joyful sounds escaping their mouths. I went on. "It was perfect. He said when he looked into my eyes, he knew I was the one. And then he proposed right then and there. He had been carrying that ring in his pocket waiting until he met his other half...ME!"

"Ming looked up with tears in her eyes all-hopeful and said, "I have that book," I smiled and continued.

"That same day we went out for coffee and had the most honest conversation I've ever had with a man. He didn't avoid a single topic. We talked for hours about love, loyalty, and having kids. And, it's been paradise ever since." My sister rolled her eyes. My mother shot me an "I never heard this story look," so I shot her an "It's my party and I'll lie if I want to" look that shut her up. After all, I was finally getting married. So she got her wish.

Ming gave me a warm hug. Luisa chimed in with a "Wait but how did he know your ring size?" I ignored her, picked up a bottle of champagne, and chugged it down.

Here's how it really went down.

On a dare from my co-worker Lizette, I signed up for one of those speed-dating booze cruises. My goal was to walk away with at least three dinner dates for the week. Thing is although the ad promised we'd find our soul mates, we had no such luck. Instead, all we met were wackos who wanted a booty call from horny bedmates.

Then, I sat across from Ray. He seemed to be pretty normal. Unlike the other candidates in the room with their pants hanging off their asses, looking like they'd just come from a Snoop Dogg concert, Ray appeared like he had his shit together. He was polite and wore a collared shirt and jeans. Best of all, he had sparkling white teeth, which is really important to me. I once dated a guy who had such bad dental hygiene that when we kissed, he gave me cavities.

During our two-minute date, when Ray pulled out a small roll of dental floss from his pocket, I knew he was the one.

The beginning of our relationship was dreamy, all I could have wanted. He was kind, funny, and attentive. We hung out every day and each time we saw one another, it was like we were meeting for the first time all over again. When we'd walk hand in hand together, it felt like we were the only two people on the planet. Our connection was out of this world. After dating only a week, we practically moved in together.

Everything was going great, until the morning he decided to burst my love bubble. After some incredible love making, Ray made me some homemade French toast. I was over the moon. Then he dropped a bomb on me. He poured himself a cup of coffee, got all serious and said, "I think we should take things slow..." I was confused.

Then he looked at me all sweet and admitted that he wasn't ready to commit. I smashed my plate on the floor and exploded. "What? Homemade French toast and morning sex is serious, bitch!" Apparently what he saw as just "hanging out," I saw as a full-blown relationship. So what if it had only been two weeks? It was the most amazing fourteen days of my life!

I believed we had something special between us, so I didn't give up. Yet whenever I asked him about our future together, he danced around the question. He'd just "talk it out" by giving me a weird massage-slash-hug as he headed out the door.

Then a couple of days later while cleaning up my place I had noticed he left his computer on. He always forgot things like keys, dinner-dates, and his mom's birthday. But when it came to his computer he had always conveniently shut it down. And he never left his phone unattended. At first I ignored the laptop and kept cleaning. Then suddenly, I ditched the broom and became like Sherlock Holmes looking for clues about his stubborn inability to commit. I was determined to make him reconsider.

I had almost given up on my search and was about to shut it down, when I looked through his sent folder, and there it was, an email, addressed to some girl named Sadie. Who the hell was that? Clearly she wasn't even Latina! I couldn't believe this Sadie and I had anything at all in common. Although he never denied being in a relationship with me, he wrote:

My lady is okay with me seeing other people. After a while, you want more than just vanilla ice cream. Will you be my Rocky Road?

Rocky Road? "What the fuck?" I thought. He was comparing me to ice cream? Boring, bland, vanilla fucking ice cream, at that? I'm like *Candy Cane Surprise*, minty and chocolaty with a luscious drizzle of fudge on top.

My heart felt crushed like nuts on a sundae. I was so pissed. A "Rocky Road" was where our relationship was headed.

To make matters worse, I found one email after another from him to meet other women. At times, it seemed like I was the accessory he'd use to bait these chicks. The hideous part was, it looked to me like they were actually turned on by the fact that he was in a so-called relationship with me. They'd say things like:

Let's shop for Cassie's birthday next week. I bet she loves Victoria's Secret. I could model some panties for you.

To which he'd reply:

Great! Thing is, I don't think I would be able to keep my hands to myself. But out of respect, I'll try. LOL.

Then he'd add a devil smiley face.

As soon as he walked through the door I threw the laptop at him. He caught it and cautiously opened it and saw what I had read. I wondered if he secretly wanted to get caught or if maybe, he was just that dumb. He looked up at me and started laughing. "It's OK, honey... see the

LOL? I was just joking. I never even went shopping that day." All of a sudden it was as if I was in a daze because even though the evidence was right in front of me, Ray had somehow convinced me none of it was what it appeared to be. That it was all one big joke. Turned out "LOL" was his get-out-of-jail card. He successfully Jedi mind-tricked me into believing he was telling the truth, so eventually I dropped the subject and let it go.

The day I finally decided to break up with him, we were shopping at K-mart. When he disappeared, I assumed he needed to use the rest-room, so I continued my search for some good sheets and colorful decorative pillows. When I couldn't find what I was looking for, I stopped to grab a latte at the K-Café and BAM! There he was hand-feeding chocolate biscotti to some 20-year-old Russian chick wearing a poncho. It wasn't even rainy outside, so I assumed she was obviously a prostitute who wore this convenient piece of clothing for an easy quickie in the restroom. I marched right up to him, threw my coffee in his face and stormed out, devastated.

For days, he kept calling my cell phone and leaving messages explaining that the reason he was hand-feeding the Russian was because she was handicapped. I couldn't believe how low he had sunk. How dare he disregard me like that? Then he had the nerve to try to turn it around on me saying that I'm the one that forced him to go shopping with me and that I also could have burned him badly. (Lucky for him it was an iced coffee that I tossed in his face.) Fed up with the bullshit, I threw him and his Sonicare toothbrush out.

Later that night while stalking his Facebook page, I saw a photo of the girl. I clicked on her profile only to find a bunch of selfies of her pouting. "Seriously?" I thought to myself. He'd leave me for that? And how the hell did she take all of these selfies? With her toes?

Sure she was pretty and a few years younger, but what else did she have going for herself? First off she wore way too much makeup. Secondly, she was obviously looking for a sugar daddy. And thirdly, this chick was so skinny she resembled a broom. I had no idea Ray had a thing for Olive Oil. "Please get this girl a cheeseburger." I whispered to myself.

As I looked at photos of her posing like a ten-year-old would on a bed overflowing with Hello Kitty stuffed animals, I was horrified to discover, before logging off, that she in fact had no arms. Ray had been telling the truth after all. I considered taking him back. I called my mom for advice.

Growing up Mommy was top notch; she had my sister and me on a schedule, cooked for us, kept the house spotless, and held down a full-time job. Yet, although I was clean and cared for, I never exactly ran to her with my problems. At times, it seemed like I could be bawling about some issue and she'd seem more concerned with getting the laundry done than wanting to listen to me. Rarely had she truly let go and enjoyed someone else's company. And though I was always nearby, it didn't make it easy to get close to her. You can't get to know a person if they constantly have their back to you dusting, mopping, or scanning the nearest surface for dirt.

I remember one Thanksgiving my family had had enough of it and Dad decided to intervene. Mom was in the kitchen cleaning a dish for like an hour. Dad busted in and was like "Put it down! It's a paper plate. " We all had a good laugh and she finally joined us for dinner.

There were times, however, when Mom did try connecting by sharing words of wisdom that she had no doubt heard from listening to radio shows while folding clothes. If I was feeling down about a relationship, she'd say things like "Well, why buy the cow, when you could get the milk for free?"

And I'd respond with, "Well, why charge for milk, when you could end up like the cow?"

At that point, she'd send me to my room, both of us clueless about what the other had said. Feeling vaguely insulted, I had to admit, my mother was right. She had warned us girls about giving too much too soon. During our breakup, Ray continued to send flowers and leave voice messages that I just ignored. As hard as it was not responding, I had to have some self-respect.

Finally, the calls stopped. And, it was really over.

I cried every day for two whole months over Ray before deciding to get on with my life.

I remembered the character Samantha Jones on *Sex and the City* once said something like, "The best way to get over a man is to get under another one." So, I took her suggestion and started dating a string of guys, rebounding from one to another, like the ball in a pinball machine.

First there was Jim. He was a very nice doctor, who swore to me he was only fifty. We met at the convalescent home I was volunteering at. He took me to matinee movies, fancy dinners at four-star restaurants, and showered me with affection, literally. He had a drooling problem. When he'd lean in to kiss me on my cheek at the end of our dates, I wound up with spit all over my face. After a while, dating him started to feel gross. Although I loved the companionship, I couldn't see myself getting serious with someone's grandpa. When I tried to imagine how having sex with him would be, I pictured him rolling on top of me and drowning me in his saliva. I broke it off immediately. I made up an excuse that I was moving to Puerto Rico. I later learned he wasn't even actually a doctor, but a resident at the home.

Then there was Steven, a good-looking African-American, who was a great kisser. Problem was, he was a narcissist. We met at the opening night of his one-man show "Bitches Ain't Shit." He singled me out at the after party and was all "Hey, I noticed you noticing me, wanna fuck?" I was shocked. I thought, "Who the hell do you think you're talking to like that?" I haven't always made the smartest choices when it came to men, especially with Ray, but for the most part, I was no skank.

This "getting under a man" thing wasn't easy. I always found some excuse not to go through with sex most of the time. Honestly it had nothing to do with me even being a saint, but more to do with me having old-fashioned Catholic guilt.

I rudely declined Steven's offer. And as I watched him walk away, I realized I sorta wanted to go home with him. I was turned on by the fact that he was so straight up about his intentions. That's the thing I admire about so-called sluts is that like the narcissist, they go after what they want and don't give a shit about the outcome. They also don't seem to get their hearts broken as often. So before I left the theater I gave him my number. After all, I was still on the rebound.

Steven made me laugh, and after kickin' it with him for a couple of months, he finally convinced me to go home with him. The sex was ri-di-cu-lous! I mean I was all over that house. He'd just confidently pick me up and tell me what he wanted me to do. "In the fireplace? Um, ok," I said with a purr. When we could no longer walk straight, I fell into his bed and went to cuddle under his arm.

Suddenly, his gray eyes gazed into mine. "Uh, wait a second sweetheart, you should sleep over there. I need my space." He pointed to a shag rug on the floor. I stared at it for a second thinking he was kidding. And then he tossed me a green Snuggie and small orange pillow with cream scrollwork, the one I was looking for at K-mart when I was with Ray. Confused, I crawled to the floor and sat there for hours humiliated as he slept all cozy in his bed. This was one of those moments where any self-loving woman would have just walked out, but I felt glued to the floor. Like I was paralyzed. I sat there until the sun came up and then walked my sorry ass home before he woke up.

After Steven, I was done with the idea of dating jerks until I met Herman. He was a hot, artsy type, and a hopeless romantic. We met at a poetry slam held at a coffee shop. I ordered a soy chai latte and while I waited for it to be made, he handed me a handwritten poem that said:

> *Your eyes are like the moon*
> *I pray under at night.*
> *Your soul shines like the stars that*

> *illuminate my dreams.*
> *I long to hold you in my arms and warm you with my burning heart.*

It was cheesy, and I loved it. The thought of someone holding me close and wanting nothing more, after being made to sleep on the floor like a dog, was enough to move me. But I noticed, after dating for a couple of weeks, that he never invited me to his house.

I wondered, "Does he have a girlfriend? Live with his mom? What is he hiding?" So I followed him home one night only to discover that he lived in his car! A two-door! I drove off and never spoke to him again. It was harsh I know, but shit, you gotta draw the line somewhere. The fucked-up thing is I probably would have stayed with him if he'd only had a four-door. If he at least had a back seat maybe, I could spend the night sometimes.

I finally gave up on the romantic idea of meeting the perfect mate and it was time to focus on my independence and myself. Despite feeling lonely, I decided to get focused on my important things to accomplish list. Things like going to yoga, listening to my Tony Robbins CD's and reading female-empowering urban books like *Do you, Boo*.

I bounced back into my normal routine of daily life. Hanging out by my lonesome never felt so great. There were days I got all dolled up for no reason. I wanted to look good for myself without worrying if I was sending a guy mixed signals. I simply wore what I wanted to because it made me feel prettier. I was having fun. I was single again and ok with it.

Then, as the universe always does when you officially decide to move forward in your life, BAM! An unexpected surprise. While folding a set of star-printed pajamas at *Sucia's*, the local laundry mat, I heard a familiar voice over my shoulder.

"Those women never meant anything to me. You're the only one I truly love. And could ever love."

I turned around and there he was. Ray looked like he hadn't slept in weeks. This cheered me up. Then he got down on bended knee right there and proposed. A tear rolled down his cheek as he opened up a small purple box.

I was stunned, speechless and slightly annoyed because I looked like shit that day. Where was he yesterday when my hair was combed? And who proposes at a laundry mat? For a second, I thought I was on one of those pranking shows and searched the ceiling and dryers for hidden cameras. When there was none to be found, I realized this was for real. I began to inspect the ring with my eyes, and then I looked at him and could see the desperation on his face. He was serious. All of a sudden the butterflies in my stomach rose from the dead. I screamed, "YES! I'll marry you!"

Maybe, he was a changed man. He was already proving he could be committed. I convinced myself that despite his faults, I was truly in love with Ray. Compared to those other guys, he wasn't really that bad. Besides I missed him. When he was with me, he was always kind and loving.

He slid the ring on my finger. It was a beautiful diamond ring. It didn't fit, sort of like us, but it didn't matter.

For that moment, I had forgiven him and was ready to move forward.

"Cut the cock already," Marianna joked as I stood over the red-velvet penis-shaped cake.

My sister Marianna was my parents' favorite child. She was once this short, plump kiss-ass. No matter how bad she was, my parents always took her word over mine in most situations. As I watched her set the cake down I couldn't help but to notice how grown up she had become. Maybe it was the booze in my system, but just thinking about how it wasn't too long ago that my little sis went from ugly duckling to super hot swan by the time she hit high school, made me get teary eyed.

The cake was a work of art, very detailed, right down to the chocolate flavored flakes that looked like pubic hairs. An unfamiliar friend of my sister's giggled as I tore the wrapping paper off a small gift box.

I didn't know what was worse, the gift she gave me, or that I couldn't remember who she was. "Crotchless panties! Have fun, girl." She teased as her and the other women squealed in approval.

Marianna pointed at the closet for my next gift. I got up walked over and opened the door. A large balloon figure popped out at me like a jack-in-the-box. "What the hell is that?" I asked, startled.

"It's a blow-up doll!" said Marianna.

"Oh, how cute. It looks like your father," Mom said examining it.

"Gross!" my sister and I said in unison.

As everyone started playing volleyball with the blow-up doll, my mom finally began to unwind. She was all smiles as she started dancing with the doll.

"I'm so proud of our girls, Juan. Look at them, they're all grown up," she said hugging the doll.

I plopped next to grandma who'd been asleep during my party. She woke up briefly and handed me a gift. "Para Ti." When I opened the box, inside were two Styrofoam breast enhancers.

Back in the day my grandma was a hot, sassy old broad who liked jewelry, perfume, and owned a pair of these handy little things that she used to tuck inside of her bras. I used to steal them and stuff them under my Underoos under shirts. They made me feel grown-up. I was touched. But when I went to give her a hug, she'd already fallen back to sleep.

My aunt Luisa was sloshed and I could tell that something was bothering her. Suddenly she yanked me by the wrist, dragged me into the bathroom and locked the door. "Did you forget about *the Curse*?" she asked somberly.

And there it was, the one thing I thought I had blocked out of my life. It was as if everything in the room suddenly went dark. How dare she bring this up the day before my wedding?

I first heard about *the Curse* from her when I was just a teen. Back then it was hard to get a straight answer about what it was and what it would do to you. I spent quite a bit of time in high school trying to avoid it all together. And after several efforts that involved Vicks VapoRub and a trip to a witch doctor, I thought I would never be faced with it again. I was afraid the mere mention of it would open up that can of worms and bring bad luck.

"I don't have the stupid *Curse*!" I snapped. Luisa opened her mouth to say something, but her eyes suddenly went blank and she blacked out. I covered her with a towel and left her in the bathroom. I knew she'd be there for the night. I had been in a good mood and hated that she'd brought it up. I needed something to take my mind off of this garbage. Just then, the doorbell rang.

"Cassandra, I think somebody is here to see you, maybe you should go see who it is," Marianna playfully teased as she pushed her boobs higher and closer together, giving her cleavage that was about to spill out of her tight sweater.

Excited, I stumbled as I ran to the door. The "Entertainment" was here. Would he be a construction worker, a police officer? I opened the door.

"An exterminator?" I shrieked in horror. Standing before me was a short, balding, chubby Dominican man. I figured that he must have had the wrong house, so I slammed the door on his face.

My sister pinched me. "Cassandra, what are you doing? That's Pepe, we already paid him."

"Are you serious?" I asked.

I had no choice but to open the door. Apparently Pepe was indeed the hired entertainment for the festivities. I decided to make the best of it and put my attention only on Pepe. After all, he would definitely distract me from this *Curse* business.

Pepe sashayed in with a big grin on his face. My grandma woke up from her nap all giddy and excitedly ran to the boom box and pressed play. Clearly she hadn't seen a penis other than the piñata in years. "Suavemente" by Elvis Crespo bounced off the walls. Pepe began gyrating his hips left and right, back and forth. He slowly approached me, sweating profusely, and then he began to circle me.

"I'm Pepe!" he pronounced as he thrust his hips towards me and patted his belly. "I exterminate roaches by day and smoke 'em by night. You must be the bride-to-be," he said, rubbing his massive belly as the stench of Old Spice and Raid emanated from his body. He grabbed me, threw me over his shoulder and spun me around the room.

After the song had finished, I jumped out of Pepe's arms and crashed dizzily onto the futon. "Woo-Hoo! I'm getting married! No more lonely nights! No more *Curse*! I'm being rescued from it all!" I exclaimed as I danced around the room with the other guests to "Head to Toe" by Lisa-Lisa. I felt nostalgic as the song brought me back to my childhood. A flurry of Polaroids flipped through my mind. I saw the boy band, Menudo; New Kids on the Block; Bobby, my second-grade beau; and Guido Gleome, my high school sweetheart. The song finished as Slick Rick's "Children's Story" swelled and blasted through the speakers. The room started to spin, and I passed out.

*I*t was chow time, now. The prison guard opened the cell and brought in a moldy peanut butter sandwich, stale chips and a rotten prostitute named Sinnamon.

"Get your fuckin' hands offa me!" she roared.

"Calm down, Sinnamon." The prison guard warned.

"What you lookin' at? I'm Wonder Woman, show some damn respect!" She hissed as she walked towards me wearing a beat up Wonder Woman costume.

When I was a kid Wonder Woman was my idol. She was smart, beautiful and kicked ass. I remember how I'd imagine her climbing in through my window and giving me her golden lasso.

I started feeling a burning and painful sensation in my pelvic area. Like a fireball about to shoot out of my coochie. Then my heart started palpitating. It was just a matter of time before it got worse. I sat in the cell staring at Sinnamon and began to comb through my childhood. Maybe if I went over everything carefully, I could uncover something I may have missed. I was sure that the key to my current predicament was rooted in the past.

Let's see, the first time I fell in love was with a kid that lived down the hall from my grandma named Bobby. He had big brown eyes and a sweet smile. Bobby was a romantic kind of kid who liked to write me poems and visit often. One time when my grandma walked away, leaving us in the living room by ourselves, he unfolded and read me a note that was tucked in his pocket.

> *Roses are red*
> *Violets are blue*
> *I like when you wear*
> *Your grandma's fake boobs.*

Bobby always read me his poetry, but something was different this time. When he looked up from reading me his latest masterpiece, he gave me a nervous glance, anxiously anticipating my reaction, like a puppy dog does when he pees on the floor. All of a sudden I threw my arms around his neck and trapped him in my grandma's bedroom. I then said the one thing a 10-year-old girl should never say to an 11-year old boy.

"Let's get married."

I blurted it out like it was no big deal, and then waited for a response. During my summer months off from school, I spent many afternoons with my grandma watching telenovelas. Therefore, I naturally assumed that when a woman declared her love to a man, he would grab her, lift her up in the air and kiss her passionately as fireworks shot off in the background. Usually, a mariachi band appeared out of nowhere to serenade the happy couple.

I stood there waiting for Bobby to profess his love to me, too. When he didn't, I got nervous and lifted my dress revealing my padded undershirt. I had hoped my peep show would make him change his mind because I'd seen it work for women on the soaps on more than one occasion. He stared at me for a second and went in for the kill.

As he groped my Styrofoam chest bulbs, suddenly my grandma busted into the room. We froze like two squirrels caught fighting over nuts in the middle of the road. She scolded, " Give me back my tetas!" Then she stormed over to me, yanked them from under my shirt, and pulled Bobby by the ear toward the front door. "I don't need those stupid things anyway. Bobby loves me without them," I cried helplessly.

"Right, Bobby?" When I turned around to face him, Bobby was long gone.

Later that day I ran out into the hallway only to find he was already playing with Kathy Bixby, the new older girl who lived in the building. She was a tomboy kind of kid who let him play with her toy guns. He was no longer interested in my grandma's tata's, or me.

The second time I fell in love was with those 70's

shaggy-haired detective buds, Starsky and Hutch. At the time, they were very manly male icons of sexuality, and when I couldn't decide who was hotter, I'd just grab two pillows for a cozy threesome. I may have been too much woman for Bobby, but in my fantasies, Starsky and Hutch disagreed.

*E*ventually, I got bored of grinding on my pillows and began to snoop around looking for anything that was erotic. What can I say? I was a sexually precocious, but definitely inexperienced kid. On days I was alone in the house, I'd put my Barbie dolls away and flip through the TV leaving it on the fuzzy channel, hoping I would see a blurred image of people humping on each other. When it became too hard to make out an ass cheek from an elbow, I got frustrated and longed to explore my parents' bedroom.

Then one day I got my wish. While they were out, I snuck into their room and started jumping up and down on the bed to burn off some pent up energy from too many Cocoa Pebbles. I jumped as high as I could get. All of a sudden, the bed broke and collapsed; I fell right through the frame.

I stood up and noticed something was stuck to my

leg. It was a magazine. I peeled it off and realized that this wasn't just any magazine. It was a dirty magazine, and there were a bunch of them with men and women doing it. Now the stuff I couldn't see on the fuzzy channel was in front of me on glossy paper. Asses, tits, legs spread eagle, and couples having sex in funky positions. I felt like a greedy little leprechaun who just found his pot of gold. No one was there to cover my eyes. It was all so weird but fascinating.

A few seconds later, my sister came running in.

"You broke the bed! I'm gonna tell!"

"Get out, Marianna," I demanded. I tried to gather all the magazines in my arms and push her out of the room, but she fought back and started screaming, "I'm telling Ma!"

So, I let her stay. We both picked a spot in the room to examine the pages of exposed body parts as if we were preparing for a test in an anatomy class. With every page I turned, the women in the photos came alive. We studied all the poses and started emulating them. We were getting a firsthand lesson on how to be sexy. I was determined that no longer would I be ditched for the cute girl next door.

My first lesson was with Miss November. It was a western type photo shoot; she wore chaps with nothing underneath. She held onto two toy guns, like the ones Kathy had. As I stared at her picture, she seemed to come alive. Her full lips were parted and she started to speak to me. She jumped out of a magazine photo and said in a sultry voice, "I'm Miss November from *Ass* magazine. Shoot 'em with a squirt gun and shake those buns." I shook my butt in front of the mirror.

Also, coming alive to me were the others. There was Miss April, wearing butterfly wings and body paint. "I'm Miss April. I like rainbows, puppies and men who take charge!" I struck her pose, with my butt in the air.

Finally, there was Miss May, "Lola" from China. "Your fortune is in my cookie," she squawked. I squinted my eyes just like Lola, pursed my lips, and added a high karate kick. "Hiya!"

Yeah, they were naked, but it was more than that that caught my attention. They were older, fully developed, and confident, nothing like me. I was attempting to do a split like Lola, when my sister ripped my magazine away. She had already sifted through her pile and wanted mine. We began a tug of war.

"Marianna, stop it. Go play with your coloring books!"

"I'm telling Ma," she threatened.

While we were fighting over the magazine, my parents suddenly barged into the room.

"Mom? Dad?" I shrieked. Neither of them said a word. They just looked around in disgust.

My mom looked at the magazine and gave my dad a look that could kill. As my mom calmly removed her street shoes and put them in the nearby cubbyhole, she looked at me like I was a giant germ.

My father lamely tried to deny all knowledge of the skin mags. "I don't know how those got there."

"Well, Santa Claus didn't bring them, Juan? How many do you have? Get rid of them and I better never see that in this house again."

Dad grumpily tossed his guilty pleasures in the trash and my Mom turned to me and said, "Shame on you, Cassandra, you oughta know better."

I didn't know how to respond, so I pointed at my sister. "It wasn't just me. She was looking too."

Marianna acted all innocent. "I was only teaching myself to read in Spanish," she professed. "See it says here 'Aye Papi, Aye Papi," she continued as she read aloud from *Spanish Fly* magazine. They totally bought her act and grounded me! "Not fair! You didn't punish Mariana!" My dad snatched the magazine out of her hand and chucked it in the trash.

"Go to your rooms. Both of you." He commanded. Part of me felt bad for my dad because I could tell he was bothered that we stumbled upon his stash. And yet the other part of me didn't care. After all, I was thrilled that I got a sneak peek into the adult world of sex. Mom angrily grabbed her bedroom slippers from the shoe cubby by the closet and gave us a good smack on the ass with each chancla. She looked like an over-caffeinated ninja warrior swinging away with both arms. My sister and I were too stupid to run out of the room, we just buzzed around in circles around her. When my mom got winded, she broke out with the dish gloves and Clorox to scrub down the room.

I was grounded for a month. That night I dreamt Wonder Woman climbed in through my window to rescue me.

"Cassandra you think you have problems? Why my corset is so tight, I can hardly breathe, yet I am still powerful. You wanna know why? I don't let the little things get the best of me. It's healthy to be curious about your body. Being a Wonder Woman means opening yourself up and discovering the wonder in you. Always remember: *Be true to you.*" She climbed through the window and got into her invisible plane. When I woke up, I had forgotten her lesson.

On my thirteenth birthday, although I was expecting my love and sex education to begin my aunt spilled the beans about *the Curse* instead.

Late that night, as my parents entertained the last of the relatives at my party, I was hanging out with a very drunken Luisa in the bathroom.

Luisa had a drink in one hand and a lit cigarette in the other. No matter how lit she was, or how many times she fell, that drink wouldn't spill.

"Get in here and lock the door," she said handing me her vodka tonic. "Take a sip." She ordered. Once I'd locked the door, I took the glass from Luisa's hand and sipped from it hesitantly.

"Ewww this tastes like rubbing alcohol!" I said making a yuck face as I spit it out into the sink. She laughed at me then finished it off. I sat on the toilet and stared at a big blue pair of hand washed granny panties hanging on the shower door.

"You see those panties there? My great grandma wore 'em then she passed them to me and now they're yours," she proudly confided.

"Um...no thanks. Keep 'em. I have my own panties." She handed me her vodka tonic again.

"Look, I'm gonna be straight with you. You're thirteen now, so its' time I tell you about *the Curse*." she said changing the subject.

"I already know all about it," I said confidently. "I got my period last year."

"I pray to God you aren't using tampons." She warned.

"I'm not." I lied.

Oh boy, the "Tampon Debate." This became a huge source of discussion in our family after my cousin Lucy admitted to using them as a teen. Apparently you were considered a tramp if you even touched them. Back then I didn't exactly tell my mom when it was that time of the month. I was afraid with her OCD she'd make me sleep on the slabs of cardboard for fear of staining the sheets. I will never forget the day I had no choice, but to join the club.

I was a cheerleader in junior high when I first got my period, which unbeknownst to me was actually considered my first unofficial curse. I had a heavy flow and, unfortunately, pads with wings hadn't been invented yet. Somehow my Mom found out about it, and got me a box of no frills pads that were obnoxiously huge.

I was in the locker room changing into my cheerleading uniform when Shelly, one of the girls on the squad shouted, "Look everybody, Cassandra's wearing diapers."

The other fifteen cheerleaders immediately circled around me to inspect my bulging ass. "Wait a sec. That's no diaper. That's just Cassandra's big ole' Puerto Rican bubble butt," laughed Heather.

"No, look," Suzette pointed out. "You can see the whole pad bulging from her skirt."

I ran to the bathroom mirror. My super maxi pad was thicker than my pom-poms. I was horrified. If this incident spread around school, the emotional scars of this situation would ruin my entire adolescent life.

I had to think quickly, so I grabbed a roll of toilet paper and dipped into the nearest bathroom stall. I removed the bulky pad and stuffed my panties, hoping the toilet paper would be less noticeable. But, when I inspected myself in the mirror again, it looked worse. I've heard of girls stuffing their bras with toilet paper, but their underwear? I finally sat on the toilet with my bloomers around my ankles and cried. I was worried I'd be the only cheerleader forced to wear pantaloons under my skirt just to hide this mess.

A few minutes later, Corey, my close friend and co-captain of the squad, saved me. She stood on the toilet seat in the stall next to mine and peeked her head over the divider. She was the only one that knew the real reason I was afraid to use anything other than pads.

"Your mom's a whack job for convincing you that this little thing is gonna make you lose your virginity. It's not," she swore. "So use it already," she said, handing me a super-sized tampon. I grabbed it then stared at it. I wrinkled up my nose in a silent "Que?"

"Take it. Stick it in!" she demanded.

I could hear the other girls from the squad by the door.

"What are you, chicken? Do it already we gotta go!" someone shouted.

I felt like I was being hazed into the "Tampon Society." All the girls began to chant, "use it, stick it, use it, stick it."

"Look, Cassandra, it will feel like a finger at first, and then after a while you won't even feel it," Corey said firmly. This was a very uncomfortable decision for me to make. In the background Boys II Men's "Motown Philly" played. It was time to get on the bus for the game. It was either the tampon or an entire roll of scratchy, sandpaper-like toilet sheets. I took the tampon out of the wrapper, took a deep breath and inserted it. It felt a bit painful at first, and then the discomfort went away. A wave of relief washed over my body as I realized that not only would this thing keep me dry, but that I was also still a virgin. Phew! Best part was, I no longer looked like I was wearing Depends under my short cheerleading skirt. I've been hooked on the cotton plug-ins ever since.

"Hey snap out of it," Luisa said, pulling me out of my

daydream. "I'm not talking about the *Red Sea*, or *Shark Month*. I'm talking about *the Curse of the Blue Vagina*."

It sounded the same to me. I told her I had learned all about vaginas as part of sex education class in the 7th grade. I realized this had to be my family's version of the famous "birds and bees" talk and I wasn't having it, so I turned to let myself out of the bathroom, when she said, "Cassandra, you're cursed."

She kept on mumbling something about love and pain and how to break the spell, but she didn't know how. I couldn't make sense of what she was trying to say because she was so drunk she was slurring her words. Was this happening because I secretly used tampons?

"Look I'm gay, so I never got it, but I think my ex got it after we broke up, so who knows? What will happen is, one day you'll just be walking and PLOP, it'll fall right out."

She was talking as if she was channeling messages for me from beyond. When she got intoxicated, she started "speaking truth." She might not make sense, but if you wrote down what she said and looked at it a few days later, it all became clear. My aunt Luisa was a wise woman in a borracha's body (a *drunk woman's* body).

I leaned in and paid attention to what she was saying, trying to figure out how much was storytelling bullshit, how much was Nostradamus stuff to be decoded, and how much was pure, liquid fire burning a hole in her brain.

As I sat on the toilet listening to her, I became terrified. I had no clue what she was talking about or how this could possibly affect a girl who hadn't even had her first real kiss yet, let alone sex. I was looking forward to becoming a woman and going to high school, but not this... Was I doomed to lose my hoo-hoo while walking down the aisle at the grocery store one day? I imagined walking down the aisle at Pathmark when SPLAT! It would fall out. In a panic, customers would surround me petrified. An employee would shout over the loud speaker, "Darnell, cleanup on aisle seven, someone lost their punani."

Luisa passed out in the tub with a lit cigarette in her hand. I guzzled the last of her vodka tonic and stared at the blue granny panties.

My aunt Luisa, who is my dad's sister, was popular in our family because when she was only 7 years old, she announced she was a boy stuck in a woman's body. Our grandparents were horrified so they called Father McDonald, the local priest, for an emergency exorcism. He came over for a pretty hefty donation and started chanting some prayers in Latin that ended with little Luisa being dunked into some holy water to get rid of the male spirit that supposedly had taken over her soul. After the exorcism, Father McDonald, had a cup of café con leche and piece of biscocho (*cake*) with the family and declared that Luisa was saved.

Just to be sure though, after Father McDonald left,

my grandparents left her soaking in a tub of salt and holy water.

Once little Luisa was all cleaned up and ready for bed, she barged out of her room with dolls in hand and dumped them in the trashcan. Then she turned to her parents and said "I'm not possessed, I'm a homo. Good night!" It was then that my grandparents threw up their hands and just accepted who she was.

As Luisa got older, she developed some spiritual gift. Maybe the salt and the holy water had something to do with it. There were times I would visit her as a youngster only to find her sitting at her kitchen table reading tarot cards for her crazy neighbors. She was very superstitious and had a ritual for everything and wore *Agua Florida* as her signature perfume.

I sat on the toilet perplexed that Luisa couldn't give me some ritual to break this so-called *Curse*. Just then I got a whiff of something burning. The flame from her ciggy had migrated to the plastic shower curtain. I ran out of the bathroom screaming, "Mom, Dad, call the fire department!" Luisa woke up for a split second and looked at me with laser-beam like eyes.

"You see, it's *the Curse*... You did this. It's all gonna go wrong for you over the next thirty years." Luisa burped as my dad grabbed her and tossed her over his shoulder. We evacuated the apartment.

From that moment on, every time I'd try to get answers from my aunt, something always happened. Either the phone rang, and it was the police saying one of my relatives had been arrested or it was the hospital saying someone had been run over. I promised myself I'd never bring up *the Curse* again. So, I had no choice but to look to my friends in high school for the answers.

Mimi Giannetti was my best friend in high school. She was an Italian spitfire who had answers to any sex question you had. Mimi always carried her Walkman around playing songs full blast through her headphones. During lunch as she snapped her fingers to the rhythm of "Candy Girl" by New Edition, I pulled off her headphones so she could give me some solutions to my problem.

"I told you already, I know what blue balls are, but I never heard of no blue vagina," she shrugged as she stuffed a ding-dong in her mouth.

"Mimi, this is serious, I have to find a cure for this thing."

"Don't worry about *the Curse*," she assured me as I unwrapped a soggy tuna fish sandwich my mother packed for lunch.

I don't know what my mother was thinking. Apparently she was trying to scare my friends away with the lunches she made me. I mean tuna sandwich with extra mayo between two slices of soft white bread and no tic-tacs packed along with it? Really? I always needed plastic gloves just to unwrap the soggy mess. Mimi felt sorry for me.

"Here have my third sandwich, I mean Jesus, you keep eating that crap and your tits aren't gonna grow," she said as she chowed down on two sandwiches at once.

"I don't have an appetite. I got my mind on *the Curse*."

"You don't even know if you have it. Calm down. Say some hail Mary's and what not."

I stared at a painting of the Virgin Mary hanging on the cafeteria wall. Although we went to Catholic high school, rarely did any of us go to confession.

"Cassie listen, I learned all about sex from watching *All My Children* and Erica Kane said in an interview once, 'you can cure anything with a glass of raw eggs or a man'." Mimi loved Erica Kane and respected any female who was overtly sexual.

"That show's been on TV forever, I think they should rename it *All Those Hags*!" I hissed.

"True! Anyway, with the school dance just around the corner finding you a guy is gonna be cake. Trust me that should fix your little problem. But girlfriend, you gotta at least let him get to second base."

I was enjoying my new lunch, and my mouth was full. I shot her a confused look. I'd become much more reserved since my days as a sexually curious kid.

"Gawd, don't tell me you don't know what the bases are all about. Don't you remember the lessons from the soaps? First base, kiss. Second base, titty rubs. Third base, he sticks his finger up your vajayjay. But you gotta be careful cause if that goes on too long he'll get blue balls which are probably way worse than the blue vag." She stuck her tongue out, hopped on the cafeteria table and started shaking her hips to attract the attention of our principal. "Mimi, get off the table or you're going to get detention," he warned.

Mimi had a crazy crush on Principal Dobez. She loved his red hair and commanding presence. In other words, she loved getting detention.

"Screw you, Principal Dobez!" she retaliated, thrusting her hips a few more times before hopping down. She got detention.

After a few weeks of staring at Principal Dobez's green eyes, she was over him and ready to move on. She decided it was better to be the one being lusted after than the one with the dopey, dreamy expression. Besides, her record couldn't take another demerit.

*I*t was a nice fall Friday evening when Mimi and I arrived at our first school dance. A banner hung on the wall that read "Funky!"

As a group of us teens all clumped together to dance, Principal Dobez took the stage.

"Welcome to your first school dance, Funky Fall Disco."

The crowd groaned at the name of the dance chosen for us by the teachers. It was a poor attempt at being cool.

"We have a surprise for you!" Dobez exclaimed. "We pride ourselves on providing you with the best culture our community has to offer. So, here to perform her latest song, please give a warm welcome to Chulupa Jones."

A flash of lights circled the small stage in the center of the gym. Chulupa Jones entered and struck a pose as her music played. She was a skinny up-and-coming artist who resembled a drag queen in really cool clothes. She wore black leather pants, a colorful top, and chains that wrapped around her waist. Her hair was sprayed pink into a perfect Mohawk.

She grabbed the mic from the stand and shouted, "Come on, kids, put your hands together. This is high school. This is where your life begins.

"Wow, I remember when I was in this school," she screamed. "All I could think about was stardom and freedom! I sat right at the back of Miss Barnaby's class. Is she still here?"

Chulupa scanned the crowd and spotted old, haggard Miss Barnaby.

"Oh my God, Miss Barnaby is that you?" asked Chulupa. "Miss Barnaby is older than Jesus! What happened to your other eye?"

A shocked Miss Barnaby touched the patch over her right eye.

The music swelled as Chulupa passionately sang the following lyrics to her wacky song:

> *Now that you're my ex-boyfriend,*
> *I'm ready to heal my heart.*
> *'Cause I don't care about you anymore,*
> *or your cat or even your car.*
> *So just step back,*
> *'cause you told me I was fat.*
> *Oh, you said I was fat.*
> *Now I go to the gym twice a day,*
> *and you just won't go away...*

She finished with a couple of *Flashdance* turns and struck a pose when the music ended.

One student shouted, "Your songs suck!"

She screamed back, "Screw you zit face! Helen, bring me a towel!" Her back-up dancer, Helen, quickly ran to her and handed her a dirty towel as the lights went out. Then, Chulupa jetted off the stage.

Mimi leaned into me and said, "The only thing dope-on-a-rope about her is that she has something you don't—style."

I had to admit, she looked good in bright colors. I was in what looked like a stylish version of one of my mother's *Bata's (dusting housedresses)*. Unlike most kids, I voted to wear a school uniform in junior high and was grateful we wore uniforms in high school. At least that way people wouldn't notice that my mom picked out my outfits from the church clothing basket. So obviously when it came time for events outside of school, I needed a little help in the dress up department.

"So what Mimi. What I lack in style, I will just make up in dance moves."

I pranced to the center of the dance floor as the deejay played Chaka Khan's song, "I Feel for You." There I confidently showed off my sexy new dance moves that I had worked on in front of the mirror.

In my mind, I was the best dancer in the room. I did the "Robot" followed by the "Kid 'N Play" dance from the movie *House Party*, where two partners do the equivalent of a kind of pat-a-cake with their feet instead of their hands. And I finished my moves off with the "Wop", where you stand with your legs still and start to worm your upper body forward and then up and down. I even threw in some pop-locking and solo break-dancing. Finally, I ended powerfully with the "Jumping Cockroach", where you stand with both legs together and duck left and right as if trying to avoid being crushed. (It was my own made up dance and I was proud.) Mimi charged at me and yanked me off the dance floor.

"Holy shit, Cassandra! Are you serious about breaking *the Curse*? You're never gonna get a boyfriend moving like that. You gotta sex it up if you're gonna have a chance. You gotta compensate, know what I'm sayin'? Watch and learn."

"I Wanna Have Some Fun" by Samantha Fox was the next song to play. Mimi started teaching me some moves and I followed along.

I swayed my hips back and forth, and caressed my body like Madonna did in all her music videos. Then, from the corner of my eye, I noticed someone watching me.

"Oh snap, Mimi, it's working. There's a cute guy moonwalking in this direction," I pointed out.

Vanilla Ice's "Ice, Ice Baby" blared through the speakers as an adorable short Italian guy moon-walked toward me. Suddenly a crowd formed around the blonde kid and he began to breakdance. After he finished he hopped onstage and grabbed the mic. Even though there were other girls around, I knew he was just talking to me.

"What up everyone it's me, Guido Gleome," he broadcasted. "The new Nilla Wafer rapper. Ha-ha, get it? Vanilla Wafer? I'm Nilla Wafer fools." Some kids began to groan. He cut them off with, "I'm serious, I'm a rapper, for real. I wrap packages at UPS after school kinda like a part-time job."

The crowd laughed.

"And I can kick some serious beats for real, son. DJ hit it."

LL Cool J's instrumental version of "I Need Love" began to play and he made up his own lyrics to my favorite song:

*When I'm alone in my room,
I sit and play wit my dick.
And in the back of my mind,
I hear my mama call,
telling me, I need to stop and
clean up my mess.
For the first time in my life
I think I need sex.
There I was hanging
with my boys in the hall.
When I saw you walk pass,
my mouth fell to the floor
I thought, damn, her lips look soft as a dove.
If they wrap around my dick,
I think I'll be in love.
I need sex.*

The crowd cheered and laughed as Mr. Dobez pulled Guido off stage by his hoodie.

His beautiful brown eyes were locked only on me. I wanted him to pull me close to him.

I followed him through the crowd. All of a sudden Mimi pulled me away and dragged me into a dark supply closet.

"Holy shit, Cassandra. I just saw sparks shooting from your crotch." I shook my head in disbelief.

"Don't you smell something weird? Something burning?"

"Sort of." I shamefully admitted.

All of a sudden I could see little lights were visible just above the floor, like fireflies. Then more of them began to shine in the darkness. Luckily no one accept Mimi noticed any of my fireworks. And even though the burnt smell didn't travel beyond a couple of feet, you could hear the sizzle of electricity.

"You're like nuclear or something! Does it hurt? Does it feel good? Did you have like an orgasm?" Mimi prodded.

"Shhh! It's *the Curse*! Please don't say anything." As soon as I said it I almost felt possessed. I started twitching and sweating for no reason at all. At one point, I could have sworn I felt something trip me. Or maybe it was just Mimi.

"You're right, this is pretty serious Cassie. Remember what I told you? A glass of raw eggs or a man."

I hadn't said anything to Mimi, but I had already tried the eggs remedy. It didn't prevent this from happening. I ran out of there with my sweater around my waist to muffle any remaining sparks, but I was afraid it might catch on fire. This energy was the most intense energy I had ever felt. I may have been just a horny teenager, but I was still frightened. It's like my body had turned into a V-2 rocket. What if I just took off and exploded right there on the dance floor? I was determined to get to the bottom of this BV nightmare before this ruined my adolescent life.

The next day, I lied and told my mom I was going into the city with Luisa and instead took a subway into the Bronx to meet, Don Miguel Lazaro. I had heard about him through one of Luisa's girlfriends. If word of this visit got to my Catholic folks, I'd be grounded for life.

I met Don Miguel Lazaro in this small Botanica deep in the Bronx. He read my tarot cards in the backroom. According to him, breaking *the Curse* was gonna take some serious work. He wanted me to try a special remedy first before we even got into the list of sacrifices I just couldn't bear to make. It was like a super involved ritual that involved me collecting dirt from a church, a cemetery, Victoria Secret shop, and the most important ingredient, water from *Santa Maria's fountain*.

Once I had collected the different kinds of dirt I needed, I was supposed to mix them all together, add some flowers, perfume and say some bedtime prayers to Saint Jude. Then at the strike of midnight, I had to light a purple candle, wash with these items and then lay in a tub full of salt water. Each item was crucial to the concoction and could not be substituted. There was only one problem. Don Miguel's assistant reminded him that *Santa Maria's fountain* no longer existed. I was screwed.

He sat there silently. After he had rubbed me down with some oils, I felt worse. He shrugged his shoulders and after a pregnant pause, suggested I use Vicks VapoRub to ward off evil spirits. He also suggested I stay away from grandma's rice and beans, (supposedly they make my symptoms stronger.) He then leaned into me and whispered in Spanish, "And if that doesn't work, get yourself a novio (*boyfriend*).

I was utterly confused. I went home and tried rubbing some Vicks VapoRub down there that I found in the medicine cabinet. It stung so bad I thought for sure I'd burned my flower off. I immediately soaked myself in the tub to take the pain away. Evidently that wasn't gonna work. But one thing was certain, if Don Lazaro and Mimi were right, then I needed to get a serious make-over to attract a boyfriend. After all, if I was gonna light up a room I wanted it to be because I looked hot not because my vagina was igniting.

The following Saturday morning, I had convinced my mother to take me to get my haircut. I had imagined making a special trip into New York City on the train and strolling into a classy salon on Fifth Avenue where Alyssa Milano's celebrity hairstylist would embrace me and style my hair.

But instead, my mom took me to Fantastic Sal's Salon. The last time I was here was when I was about five years old and she took me to get my first bowl haircut. While the ladies gossiped with my mom as she got her hair washed, I decided out of sheer boredom, to swallow a penny I'd found on the floor I wanted to see if I would poop it out later. The problem was the penny ended up getting lodged in my throat. In an effort to save my life, Kazan, the salon owner grabbed me by the ankles and shook me over the sink until it flew out of my mouth. All the hairstylists cheered.

We never went back until today. Once inside the salon, a tall, middle-aged woman with glasses and frosted hair approached me. It was Kazan, she looked exactly the same.

"Welcome back to Fantastic Sal's," she greeted warmly. "Why Cassandra, I haven't seen you since you were only knee high. Uh-oh ladies, hide your loose change," she laughed.

I looked around the place. It resembled a bingo parlor at the local church. The customers were so old that the women seated on salon chairs next to mine could have attended high school with Moses himself. A while later, a young, hip-looking teenage girl walked in with her mother. She had cool feathered shoulder-length hair. Her mom, on the other hand, had one of those soccer mom bobbed haircuts that every woman seems to get after the age of forty.

I waited patiently to see which stylist the teenage girl would choose to do her hair. Then she said, "Okay, Grandma, I'll be back to get you when I'm done at the mall." As she walked out the door she smacked her gum loudly and laughed in my face.

"Oh no! I don't wanna look like a soccer mom," I pleaded.

"You won't," mom reassured me. "Things have changed around here."

I sat in the chair and pulled out a folded magazine photo of Alyssa Milano. I had to be certain that Kazan, with her multi-layered, short Luke Skywalker haircut, knew exactly what I wanted.

"Uh-huh, so you want to look like Alyssa Milano? I can do that," Kazan promised me. "Why you kids nowadays are trying to look ten years older is beyond me. Take a seat."

I wanted to say "Kill me now!" as she decided between the Suave and the VO5 shampoo for my hair. I looked around to see if I could spot the chic shampoos in normal hair salons. "Do you have any Nexus or Paul Mitchell hair washes?" She ignored me.

"Joann, did you hear what happened to Leslie?" Kazan asked a nearby stylist while she sudsed up my hair. "On her way to the post office, she spontaneously combusted. POOF! Gone right there on the spot. All that was left of her was a big blue smear and one of her shoes. Rumor had it she was cursed." I began to feel an uncomfortable tightness in my *palomita*. Was she referring to *the Blue Curse,* as in the *Curse of the Blue Vagina* that I assumed only ran in my family?

A bead of sweat dropped from my forehead as I leaned in closer, listening intently.

"It's that feeling of emptiness you just can't shake. Look who's talking though, I may end up just like her. My love life stinks, too." I sat there hoping that wearing tighter panties could keep my symptoms at bay. Kazzan went on.

"Anywho, that blind date I met last week was awful.

I mean I didn't care that he was missing his hands, but when he didn't pick up the check, forget it!" The girls behind the counter sounded like a pack of howling hyenas. I could see chunks of my hair falling to the floor with every giggle that came out of her mouth. When Kazan finally finished cutting and blow-drying my hair, she spun my chair around to face the mirror.

"There you go, kid. Just like you wanted, Julie from *The Love Boat*. All done," she smiled as she undid my smock.

I was horrified! She had turned me into a soccer mom after all. I examined my puffy new bobbed haircut in the mirror.

"But I don't look like Alyssa Milano—or anyone hot," I whimpered.

My cheeks turned bright red, and my eyes began to water.

"Twelve bucks, kid," she said, holding out her hand.

My mom came in as I was handing over the cash. "Cute! You could be a librarian with that hair. I love it," mom complimented as she pulled out a coupon from her purse and handed it to Kazan.

"Oh, would you look at that. Today's cut is on the house. Enjoy." Kazan said as she waved good-bye.

God forbid my mother actually paid full price for anything. Now I know why she was so enthusiastic about taking me to that particular salon. I left the salon looking like a boy with a mushroom head.

That Sunday I visited my aunt and when she opened the door, she stared at me in disapproval. "What the hell did they do to your hair?" Luisa asked as she circled me and picked at my hair. I immediately burst into tears. I felt like I had a head full of lice.

"This is why you gotta go to the Dominican salons. They do everything. They may burn the hell out of your scalp, but it's worth it cause no matter what, your hair always comes out STRAIGHT."

I knew if I showed up to school with my hair the way it was, it would not only ruin my social life, but Guido wouldn't even look my way. I imagined myself as the newest cast member, "Fern," on Little House on the Prairie. "Pa, can I go out and play with the other kids?" I'd beg Michael Landon. "Not today, Fern, we need to keep you in the house until your hair grows back."

"Don't worry. We'll fix this," my aunt interrupted,

transporting me back to reality. She was surprisingly gung-ho. I guess I was like a doll for her to play with. She could appreciate beauty but had never really indulged her feminine side.

I walked with her into the bedroom where all kinds of hair and face products sat on her vanity. "These belong to my girlfriend. They work for her. Pass me the Aqua Net," she said as she pulled out some scissors and a pair of clippers and snipped at my hair.

"You'll never break *the Curse* if you look like an electrocuted poodle," she informed me. I hoped she wouldn't pass out during my second makeover. I couldn't risk my hair catching fire. As she worked furiously, she kept a ciggy dangling between two fingers.

She buzzed, sprayed, and teased.

"Now you just need a little makeup. Let's see if I can find something natural."

She searched the vanity, pulling out drawers until she found the perfect colors for me. "Aha, here we go, bright neon orange lipstick and fuchsia blush." When she finished my hair and makeup, she looked me over, and I could tell by the look on her face I was missing something. Luisa's girlfriend was a petite girl in her early twenties who wore a small shoe size, so everything fit.

"In order to look good and get a man, you need to dress like our Latina freestyle Sistas: Exposé, The Cover Girls, Chulupa Jones."

They were all fabulous Latin superstars who had

everything: confidence, beauty, and money. And they attracted men everywhere; all because of the way they wore their hair. She was right. This was the funky street pop look I was going for all along. Freestyle music is to Puerto Ricans what Bob Marley is for Jamaicans and potheads; timeless. To this day, middle-aged Puerto Ricans still groove to these classic sounds.

"Don't worry, you're gonna walk out of here looking and feeling like Lisa-Lisa herself when I'm done with you."

Finally, Luisa covered my eyes with her hands. The finishing touch was a spritz of hair glitter. When she pulled her hands from my face, I was standing in front of a cracked full-length mirror. I almost started to cry, but this time they were tears of joy. I loved my new look. My soccer mom hair had been improved dramatically. It was now shorter from the crown up to the top and buzzed on the sides, with bangs covering one eye. I left my aunt's looking and feeling great from head to toe, complete with hot pink lip-gloss, purple Maybelline mascara, and a bag of updated clothing from her girlfriend.

Monday morning I stopped by Mimi's on my way to school. When she opened the door to greet me she was stunned by my transformation.

"Jesus! I can't bring you into my house looking like that. My parents won't believe you're Italian." I rolled my eyes. Ever since Mimi's sister Merie hooked up and eloped with Julio, her parent's mechanic, Mimi's folks swore off all Latinos. For some reason, they always assumed I was Italian and Mimi went along with it. She bolted out of the house with a "Bye see ya later," to her folks and we were on our way.

Once at school, I re-applied some more lip-gloss then searched my purse for some Now & Later candies and when I looked up, there he was. Guido walking hand in hand with Tomeka Jones! My heart sank. "Mimi, when did they start going out?" She shrugged her shoulders. I sadly walked to my locker and put my book bag away.

Tomeka was a tall, beautiful, African American girl with perfect chocolate skin who wore a very expensive long-haired weave that almost looked real. To make matters worse, she was also the captain of the drill team, which meant she could out-dance me any day.

Even though many students complimented me in the hallway on the way to my classes, I kept to myself for the rest of the day. I sat in study hall with my headphones on and played the instrumental version of "Every Rose Has Its Thorn," by Poison. I pulled out my notebook and wrote out my own lyrics:

The words pierced my soul,
I felt my heart skip a beat.
Was it something I said or something I did?
Are my colors not bright enough?
I tried to forget this, but I just can't deny–
my new style was just for you.

In my hair I wear 'Dippity -Do'.
I got on fuchsia lip-gloss,
'Exclamation' perfume,
I just wanna be wit you!

After school instead of taking the bus, I walked home alone. My pity party was interrupted when Guido suddenly pulled my earphones off my head. "Hi, I been meaning to talk to you for a long time, I'm Guido."

I stared deeply into his big brown eyes and time seemed to disappear. I wanted to kiss him but didn't want to get killed by Tomeka. He leaned into my neck and inhaled the scent of my perfume. He was so cute I could hardly contain myself. "Ah-ha *Exclamation* perfume. My old aunt Lucy wears that sometimes." I was thrilled. The closest any boy had come to touching me was when my cute cousin Gary swatted a mosquito on my arm. I felt chills all over my body. It seemed as though there was a glimmer of hope for the two of us after all.

"Me and Tomeka just broke up."

"But you guys looked so happy today."

"Yeah, whatever. She acts like I ain't good enough for her, so I'll need a new girl who can shake that ass, to come with me to the next dance." I was confused, our school only had three dances a year, and we'd just had the first one. The other wasn't happening until the spring, which was months away.

"You wanna go with me?" he asked charmingly. But there was a catch—he wanted me to join the drill team!

After all he had his status to think about and he couldn't just go with anybody to the dance. Not even somebody with great hair. "You got great moves. Show people what you can do."

I nodded eagerly. He was so right. But, of course, I'd have to go through Tomeka to make the team. And she was gonna have it out for me, fo' sure.

That Thursday, when I showed up for drill team try-outs, it was like she'd been warned. Tomeka eyed me as I slinked to the back of the bleachers and motioned to one of the other girls to hit play on the boom box. Then, she demonstrated what they were looking for to the pulsing, pelvic-pumping sounds of Bell Biv Devoe's song "Poison."

We saw a posse of teen girls getting their freak on. Eight girls spun around in perfect pirouettes. Then they thrusted their pelvises in sync with each other. I felt like I was an extra on the latest Janet Jackson music video, watching their hot routine as they squatted and came forward with their arms jerking outward like they were rowing a canoe. For the finish, they leaped, cartwheeled, and tumbled their way across the gym.

Tomeka gestured for the audio tech, Javi, to cut the music. She tossed her hair back and strode to the center. She stood there for a minute, sizing us up. She just shook her head like it was hopeless. "Okay, people, get up! We're gonna walk you through the beginning…"

After about an hour, Tomeka didn't even try to disguise that she had it in for me. "Okay, you can't just knock people down carelessly and call that dancing, Cassandra!" she yelled. "Do it again."

A group of us performed the routine. And she made my group repeat the routine over and over again. "Five, six, seven, eight. Again! Five, six, seven, eight…"

By the nineteenth time, I had it down. Mimi stood up on the bleachers and cheered me on. Tomeka looked at the clock. "I have a hair appointment, so we gonna do this one more time, and then we pick the girl that is gonna be down wit us."

Something came over me as I danced my last time performance that day. With focused determination, I imagined being on stage with Madonna as one of her backup dancers. The spotlight turned on me, and I not only did the routine but also added my own spectacular moves. When it was over, I snapped out of my trance to find Tomeka and the other girls on the team frozen, staring dead-at me. On the floor around me, all of the other dancers were knocked out cold. Tomeka looked at me with an evil grin on her face.

"That just wasn't good enough. You're cut."

I was mortified. Tomeka defeated me. As I gathered my belongings to leave, the current drill team formed a circle around Tomeka next thing I know, Julia a large African American girl, who was also the co-captain, pushed her aside and came over to me.

"Cassandra, you did a good job. You knocked everyone out but still kept up with the routine, it shows you're tough and can keep it moving. So that makes you one of us. Congratulations, you made the team." Tomeka was outnumbered. She sucked her teeth and walked away.

Unbeknownst to me, Guido had joined Mimi on the bleachers. He shouted, "That's my girl!"

Tomeka turned and looked at him and then turned to me and laughed. "Oh, so you're his girl now? Good luck with that," she said sarcastically.

I walked over to him, as some girls congratulated me. He met me halfway. We reached each other and remained silent. There was nothing else that needed to be said. I knew he liked me, he'd just announced it for everyone to hear. Our feelings were mutual. And then we kissed! It was my first real kiss and it was amazing. Suddenly sparks exploded from my pelvic area like it was the Fourth of July in my pants.

Through the intercom, I could have sworn I heard the song "Electric Boogie" by Marcia Griffiths. I walked through the halls imagining the entire student body doing the electric slide in my honor.

Late that night while on the phone with Guido, I noticed I was still burning down there. It was painful, but I was also kind of proud. I felt I had an adult burden. A great secret I had to keep from my mother. I actually thought I even saw a small black circle singe the sheets over my lap. A scarlet letter "O" shaming me, marking me.

I could hear my mother's chancletas padding down the hall. Suddenly, the footsteps stopped outside my door. I tried to muffle the phone, but I could still hear Guido's voice from under the sheets. I squeezed the phone between my thighs. I uttered an involuntary sigh, as I felt a slight vibration from the phone. Mom barged into the room.

"Who are you talking to at this hour of the night?"

"Nobody, I mean I was just praying to Jesus." I denied as I clasped my hands together and continued my false prayer.

"And don't let the bed bugs bite, Lord Jesus."

Mom wasn't falling for it. She could see I wasn't on my knees and the covers were swirled around me suspiciously. She marched over, saw my red face, and followed the phone cord leading under my blankets.

She grabbed it from me. Lucky for me she assumed it was Mimi on the other end of the line. "It's after 8, you know the rules Mimi. Cassandra can't talk on the phone. You'll see her tomorrow in school!" She slammed the phone on the receiver, unplugged it and took it with her as she left my room. If she'd known I was really talking to Guido, she would've whipped out the chancla. But deep down inside I didn't care that I was disobeying her or breaking silly rules. Talking to Guido felt so electrifying. I popped the mixed tape Guido made for me into my cassette player and fell asleep with my headphones on listening to Salt n Pepa's "Let's Talk about Sex." I was in love for the first time.

"I sparked when I was with Guido." I confessed to Sinnamon as she braided my hair in our jail cell. Maybe it was his high-top Adidas, or the sound of his voice. Or maybe it was that loud romantic music from his boom box he'd serenade me with as we rode the bus home from school. To this day, every time I hear music by Jodeci, Keith Sweat, or Guy, it still sends a chill up my spine.

During that period in my life, I was having so much fun just being in love. At times it seemed as if I'd beaten *the Curse* because I had a new sense of self-confidence. I wasn't just Cassandra with the cool clothes that were just hand-me-downs. I was Cassandra, the hot new freshman with her senior beau.

I remembered how my body was responding to all this passionate energy I was experiencing. Sometimes I felt like I was floating on clouds. Other times it was like

I was at war with myself. And when that happened, I felt like I was being zapped from the inside out. But at least, I finally had an enemy, something to fight. No longer was I just slogging through life, waiting to become an adult, so I could finally leave, and become a grown-up.

It was when I felt most confident that *the Curse*'s physical sensations actually felt great. But when Guido let me down and I started to doubt myself, then *the Curse* morphed into a dark cloud that fogged up my mind leaving me in physical pain.

I was on an emotional roller-coaster ride going from happy to sad based on his mood at any given time. It would drive me crazy. My brain would go on slow-mo making everything more complicated than it was. I couldn't make the smallest decisions like whether or not I should super-size my meal.

This is how I came to feel in most of my adult relationships. This kaleidoscope of feelings based on whatever was going on with my partner. It was a theme that followed me from high school up until I got locked up.

It's hard enough being a teenager for the first time, let alone having to deal with this BV crap. Why had God or some loco curandero cursed my Nuyorican sisterhood? At the time I blamed Guido, who could sometimes be a dick. After all, he was causing the worst symptoms of *the Curse*.

"I started bending over backwards just to please him, to be loved by him. And I still do that in my relationships with guys, to this day," I admitted.

"The shit we do for dudes." Sinnamon acknowledged.

On my sixteenth birthday, since my parents never threw me a quinceañera at fifteen, I assumed they would at least throw me a surprise sweet sixteen party instead. But when my father suggested we stop at McDonald's to celebrate, I realized they had nothing planned at all. So out of guilt, they caved in and gave me permission to go to the movies with Guido.

I had put on my new hot pink dress from *Contempo Casuals* and applied a fresh coat of electric blue Maybelline mascara. Then I smoothed on some bubble-gum flavored lip-gloss (for a night of making out.) I was all dressed up ready and waiting for him to scoop me up an hour before he was due to arrive. I waited and waited, hoping one of the many cars that passed by our front window, was a beat up gray Toyota Tercel that Guido sometimes borrowed from his stepfather.

After a long while of patiently waiting, I felt a sinking

feeling in my stomach.

"Look, your stupid boyfriend isn't coming," my sister declared.

As I got more anxious about Guido possibly not showing up, my family grew increasingly irritating. Every time I thought they were going to leave me alone, they sprang up like microwaved popcorn.

My sister started singing, "No one loves Cassandra! No one loves Cassandra!"

"Shut up, Marianna!"

Aggravated, I called out to my father to help me. "Dad, will you say something?"

"Just don't come home pregnant," he warned.

"Ugh! All of you go away. It's my birthday!" I stayed glued to the front window. I watched the sun go down and the stars pop out. It was getting later and later, but I still kept waiting, hoping to be rescued by my *Knight in Shining Armor*.

Hours passed and eventually my family grew tired of teasing me and just let me be. I felt a deep pain in my heart. I started crying quietly. At around midnight, my father stood silently next to me, waiting as tears rolled down my cheek. With sadness, he put his hand on my shoulder and pulled me away from the window. He didn't say much, just wiped my tears away and walked me upstairs to my bedroom.

That's the thing about my pop; he is always there. Even though we never talked about *the Curse*, somehow having him with me at that moment made me realize that if he could stand by my mom no matter what, then someday someone would be there for me too.

That Monday as the school bell rang, Guido came running toward me.

"Cassandra, I'm so sorry, my car broke down."

I ignored him. He hadn't made an attempt to call me the entire weekend. So as far as I was concerned, he was officially cut off. It was over. I felt that now that I was a 16-year-old woman, I needed to have some self-respect.

I walked down the hall and felt sick to my stomach. I was scared about what the future held. Would this pain go away? It grew from a pain "down there" to a deep pain in my chest. This was my first breakup. My heart felt like it was broken into a million pieces. My punani felt like someone had kicked me in the nuts a million times. "Ahhhhh!" I yelled as I punched my locker.

Two weeks later, when it came time for the spring dance, I went alone. The gymnasium was filled with dozens of colorful blue and silver balloons. With mounting fury, I watched Guido and Tomeka dancing. I had to find a replacement fast. I quickly turned in a panic to my classmate Peter.

"Quick, Peter, dance with me." He looked at me as if I was nuts. "I don't care if you're in a wheelchair. I'll use a folding chair. Let's go. Please?"

He rolled his eyes and wheeled himself away.

"Fine, be that way!"

I found Mimi and tried pulling her off the dance floor to give me advice. That's when she told me off. "You know what? For months now, you've been pushing me aside. You seem to only want to talk to me when you have a problem, and I'm sick of it. When you got me this charm with half a heart that said 'Best Friends Forever,'

I took that seriously. Go dance by yourself."

I was completely alone. So I took her advice and danced alone. I danced to ease the pain. I danced to prove I didn't need Guido or anyone, and I danced to keep from crying.

"Get it together Cassandra. In a few years, none of this is going to matter." I said to myself.

I smiled half-heartedly, but inside it did matter. So I stopped dancing, stood there and cried. Mimi came over and gave me a hug. I didn't feel any better.

I left the dance and went to visit my aunt Luisa.

When I arrived at Luisa's, her new girlfriend Candy was having a party of her own. The sexy beats of Prince's "Sexy Mutha Fucka" boomed through the speakers as Candy passed out a tray of appetizers. Displayed on the coffee table in the middle of the room were never-before-seen-items of pleasure for all to examine.

"What we have here is our spring panty collection. Lots of leather and lace," she announced.

When my aunt saw me hovering by the door, she rushed over to me with a glass of wine. We locked eyes. She could tell something was happening. Evidently I had been suffering from *the Curse*.

"Here, drink this and take a few deep breaths. Pay attention to Candy. You can learn a lot from her."

Candy was an ex-stripper turned entrepreneur. Luisa had agreed to let her host one of her panty parties at her place. While I found Candy's items interesting, something caught my eye.

"This next lingerie piece is my favorite." And there it was: my hero's outfit. A cross between what the women wore in the dirty magazines and Wonder Woman herself. I was mesmerized by the costume.

"The outfit comes complete with a whip in case your partner gets out of line. Cassandra, you have a pretty figure. Why don't you be my model and try it on?" Somehow she knew that this was exactly what I had wanted all along. She held it for a split second and looked into my eyes.

I knew that this moment, that outfit, whatever it was she was about to say...would change my life forever.

"The panties are edible..."

I ran to the bathroom and closed the door. I couldn't wait to become Wonder Woman. I put on the outfit. The edible panties looked like they were made out of Fruit Roll-Ups. They had melted in my hands a bit, so I licked my fingertips. It was cherry flavor, yum. I looked in the mirror and studied my newly developed body. Wow, when did I grow up? My boobs were filled in, my butt was round, my hair was long, and my skin seemed to glow. Just then Candy burst through the door to inspect my outfit. She was definitely drunk. "You are pretty! Look at you." She was looking at me funny.

As a teen, many times my aunt joked with me about how her and Candy thought I was gay "You're one of us.

Own it." Truth is, I wasn't gay, but I was horny. I envisioned how my first time having sex with Guido would be. In my mind, I saw clouds parting in the sky. Then Sheila E. appeared wearing angel wings and playing the congas as we humped to the rhythm of "Glamorous Life".

"Just have fun, explore yourself girl. Sometimes going solo is just as good." She handed me a pink vibrator. I studied this strange, light pink, banana-shaped item, then placed it on the sink. I looked in the mirror and finished my second glass of wine. All of a sudden I heard a knock on the door.

"Go away. I want to be alone." The door opened unexpectedly. I was pissed. But when I saw who was standing there, a smile grew on my face.

"Damn! You look sexy in that outfit." It was Guido.

"How the hell did you know I was here?"

"Mimi told me," he said with a smirk.

I don't know if it was because of the wine that was in my system, but suddenly I was determined to break this damn *Curse*. I refused to go on like this. I grabbed Guido, pulled him into me and we kissed passionately. That electric energy surged through my body again. "I have an idea. Let's play a little game called pony." He looked at me confused. "You be the pony and I'll get on top," I growled seductively.

We kissed and he started to feel me up. My panties were getting wet and sticky and suddenly they were a gooey mess!

"Oh, snap. Did you get your period?" he asked. He was grossed out and started washing his hands. I looked down. "Oh no, my panties melted." I was so embarrassed. As he looked at the cherry-flavored goo stuck to my thigh, I grabbed his neck and pulled him close.

"Hey, slow down. Why don't you take a shower and get dressed? I want to take you out to a fancy spot to make up for your birthday." I was bugged that he turned me down, but I was too buzzed to feel like shit.

As I washed up, I reflected on how much Guido had changed. He was no longer the cocky little player who was just about flirting. I thought about how real he was when we were alone together. I was relieved.

I wouldn't have to chase that kind of intimacy anymore. I relaxed and stopped frantically rummaging through all the clothes in my aunt's closet looking for something to impress him. I knew what I would wear, something simple and grown up. I pulled out one of Candy's more conservative outfits, a crisp pencil skirt that nipped in at the waist and a silky, blush-colored blouse.

As Guido and I sat in a booth at the IHOP, we were both aware that this wasn't just a makeup dinner. We would be saying good-bye.

There had been hints that both of us were planning for a future separate from one another. Maybe that's why the time we spent together felt so precious. But, this was the first time we discussed our plans head on.

"Well, I'm going upstate. You gonna visit me?"

"In jail?" I joked. "What if my car breaks down?"

We teased and prodded each other. Not out to hurt each other, but trying to develop the calluses that would cover the pain of moving on. We talked and laughed some more. The conversation flowed easily between us like it did when we first met. Looking back now I realize that the thing I appreciated most about Guido, was that I always felt desired by him, even when things weren't great between us. When he looked at me, it was as if he was in awe of me.

"I want you to know that no matter what, you'll always be my special girl." he said warmly.

He seemed older, more relaxed and more comfortable in his skin. As if, he'd already gone away.

"Let's meet here in five years, and if neither of us is married yet, we'll run away together and elope." I subtly proposed. He blushed, then nodded in agreement. I took that as a silent yes.

Something from within told me this night would be our last. I was well aware that most high school relationships don't last forever, unless you accidentally get knocked up. I looked into his gleaming eyes and I was finally ready to do it. After all, even though I knew this relationship was coming to an end, I'd always known I wanted my first time to be with someone I thought I was in love with.

I leaned into him and whispered, "I'm ready."

Instinctively he knew just what I meant and quickly called for the bill.

I started to believe that maybe true love could be the thing to break *the Curse*. I mean if my mom managed to escape it when she married Dad, then that had to mean there was hope for me too.

A kissing frenzy began. I was so lost in his embrace, that time and distance disappeared. Somehow we managed to go from the parking lot of the IHOP to the inside of his bedroom a few blocks away. I heard the honks of cars faintly, because I was oblivious to everything around us.

This was an empowering moment. I was going to love the hell out of him. I wanted to set my blue vagina free! The energy I felt was one of pure joy as he slowly lifted me onto the bed. I closed my eyes as he pulled up my skirt. One minute I was on the bed, the next minute I was pinned up against the wall. It felt great. We were young and enjoying our last moments together. The passion was intense and it was even better than I had fantasized.

Just as we were about to climax, he finally said the words "I love you." My vagina and I were thrilled. At that moment instead of the usual blue sparks, I saw a burst of purple. Then a light shade of violet formed around us. The spell was broken, or so I thought...

When I woke up this morning, I could hear the wedding march. I stared at my beautiful cream-colored gown. I put it on and realized I had something old, (me), something new, (the dress), something borrowed, (my mom's pearl necklace), and guess what was my something blue? MY VAGINA! It started to shoot sparks like it did in high school. How could this be? Sometimes when I got with Ray, I'd feel the old numbing or stinging sensation, but I just ignored it. After all now I was doing the right thing. I was being mature and getting married. I would be sanctifying the sex we had. So, what was the problem? What was my body trying to prevent me from doing?

I hadn't felt this way in ages. I stood in front of the mirror feeling frightened. I was young and disoriented again. Was I making a mistake by tying the knot with Ray? I sat down on the bed and began to confess to the powers that be that for the past few months Ray and I barely had sex. And this made me feel rejected and unattractive. Although I enjoyed our lovemaking, many times it seemed as though it was always on Ray's terms. It was like he was dangling a carrot on a string and I was a rabbit eager to grab it as it kept being pulled away. It was infuriating to me because as a feminine woman, I just didn't want to be forced to chase after it. And yet if I didn't, sex would never happen.

I became diffident and the only thing that gave me hope was remembering the moments Guido yearned for me back in high school. I wanted so badly to believe that if someone like Guido could feel me, then maybe others would feel the same.

Problem was that I wasn't attracted to the Alpha male that wanted sex constantly either. I had this secret battle going on inside of myself for a long time so to keep from getting hurt and feeling rejected, I held back a little part of me …again. Could that be why my vagina was blue? I didn't understand it. Had I been confusing love with sex?

I felt cut off from Ray, and always blamed myself. Deep down I craved that my body leapt ahead and betrayed my strong passions. But eventually that part of me got tucked away and turned blue. For some reason, I could never focus on the things I wanted in a partner and trust that, maybe the universe would hear my plea and correct my ailment.

Maybe It wouldn't have bothered me so much if Ray

hadn't been the kind of guy who seemed to be more interested in saving other women, rather than appreciating and loving the one he had. It was hurtful to run into these romantic flings, these objects of chivalry, time after time, woman after woman, during our relationship. Was he having sex with them? I was so perplexed. If Ray was never going to change, then maybe getting married was just something I had to check off my "to do" list.

But, what was I thinking? It's a little too late to turn back now. I ran out of the house with my wedding gown in tow hoping to clear my head. I ended up where Guido and I had our first official date. I sat at the old restaurant not too far from the chapel. To add to my despair, I recognized the same waitress who had worked there back when I was in high school.

"Welcome to IHOP. Can I take your order? We have pancakes and French toast and waffles..."

Behind me sat a happy-sounding family of three. I could hear them pleading with their fussy kid to eat.

"Now, Peter, eat the pancakes. Mommy loves you."

"No, no, I don't want it," the kid cried.

"He doesn't want it. Don't eat it, little man. It's all good, Daddy loves you."

I sat there paralyzed. I recognized those voices. I slowly turned around and there they were. Mimi, Guido, and their son Peter. I felt like I was in the Twilight Zone. What the fuck?

Mimi and Guido were together? What total bullshit!

What happened to the girl who told me time and again I could do better. And Guido always acted like he couldn't stand her.

For a second, I wanted to believe that somehow the universe orchestrated events that put us together in the same place after all these years, so that we could make good on our promise to elope with each other. And then little Peter started crying and I snapped out of that bogus daydream real quick.

I wondered how the hell this could have happened and then I went bananas. Not because Mimi and Guido were together, but because they seemed happy when I was the one that did everything right and was miserable.

"Holy shit, Cassie that you?" Guido asked. What happened next I could only conclude was *the Curse* in full effect. I leaned over the back of my booth, snatched the pancakes off of Peter's plate, and stuffed them in Mimi's mouth. Then I grabbed Peter's spork and lunged at Guido. Peter got so scared he got up from his booster seat and ran off. Guido couldn't control the snorting laugh that escaped. So, I punched him in the face. He'd gotten pudgy, which only pissed me off more, so I punched him again.

Mimi still hadn't swallowed the pancakes, her cheeks just bulged. I slapped her for good measure, and a soggy pancake flew out. Then I slapped her other cheek, left, right, left, right. For some reason, Guido didn't interfere—he ran off to find little Peter instead.

Mimi turned red from the assault. I just couldn't stop myself. She just sat there and took it. Was she in shock? She said nothing! Even when she had spat the last of the pancake out. I roared like the devil then turned to her pug nose and stuffed two sausage links up her nostrils shouting, "You like Italian sausages don't ya? Don't ya?" I was releasing all my anger from years of being the good girl plagued by self-doubt!

She started to wipe her face and repeatedly sneeze. I still hadn't had enough. I grabbed the pitcher of syrup off the table and tagged the lemon yellow walls with a "Love sucks."

Some kids started giggling. I started screaming like a madwoman. "This isn't funny! This is my life! Just look at me! It's my wedding day and I'm still cursed! My life has passed me by and here I am obsessing over my loves and old friends. It's ridiculous!"

Somewhere between the waitress, the happy fucking family, and the sound of the clock, I'd totally lost it. I walked out, grumbling to myself like a crazy, homeless person. "Why does everyone get to be happy, but me?" I screamed at the top of my lungs.

Next thing I knew, I heard police sirens from a distance. I wanted to believe they couldn't possibly be coming for me. I didn't even notice when a squad car pulled up and slowly rolled beside me.

*S*o, that's why I'm here covered in blueberry maple syrup on my wedding day." All of a sudden, when I'd finished saying all I needed to say, Sinnamon calmly came over to me and smacked me dead in the face.

"Wake up, sister. Stop placing your happiness in someone else's hands. Show some damn self-respect."

Maybe it was the smack that made me hallucinate, but when I looked up at Sinnamon, she had become Lynda Carter, a real Wonder Woman. Her weave was being pushed up by the golden tiara. Her golden cuffs circled her flabby and very tatted arms. She solemnly handed over her golden lasso to me.

Deep down I knew that *the Curse of the Blue Vagina* had nothing to do with my family, my first love, my fiancé, or anyone else. It had to do with me.

My aunt's horror story had haunted me, and every

time I heard about another woman's love troubles, I attributed them to *the Curse*. But, I was the only one who was able to give it power. I had labeled the natural urges and feelings that flooded my body as evil and it was much easier to blame it on being cursed. When I fell short of my goals or betrayed my self-worth in the name of love, as hard as it was to admit, I only had myself to blame.

I took a deep breath and let out a sigh. It felt good. The officer came by to release Sinnamon. He looked even cuter to me now. Before she left, Sinnamon turned to me and said "Just remember, do you boo." I smiled to myself and nodded my head in agreement.

I went over to the sink in the corner of the cell and splashed my face with water, and when I looked up, there sitting above the sink was a mirror. Even though my face was beet red from the slap, I smiled at my reflection. I guess I had to humiliate myself and be brought this low to be able to admit that maybe I got myself here because I believed sex was love.

When I was young, I was afraid of giving into that energy, and as an adult if I didn't give into it I didn't feel loved. I didn't have any more answers than I had that morning. But, I felt lighter and more confident anyway.

As I sat on the dirty cot in jail, staring at the iron bars I noticed a fly had gotten caught in a spider's web. The harder it tried to break free, the more entangled in the web it became. Sitting in the corner was the spider just watching and waiting until that fly was nice and trapped before it made its way to finishing it off. Finally, the fly gave up. It was time for me to give up too. Time for me to stop trying so hard to figure out what was wrong and start looking at what was right about my current situation and my life.

I was spending way too much time focusing on my past hurts and on what Ray was doing that it didn't occur to me that I was completely ignoring the things that made me happy. After a while, it just gets exhausting jumping through hoops to please a man who doesn't even realize that's what you are doing. I also started to wonder if maybe there were times where I was just too strong or demanding in my relationships and didn't know it. No man wants to be chased let alone made to feel bad if he doesn't meet my expectations.

Maybe all I had to do was stand back and take my attention off all the shit I felt Ray was doing wrong and start focusing on the qualities I desired most in a husband to be.

I thought about how I like humor, and warmth, passion, and generosity, gentleness, power, love, intimacy and yes, sex, (which is not the same as intimacy).

I thought about how I like the kind of man that will give me a look and just understand that maybe all I need is a hug. Or if that isn't what I need, then instead he'll become like a caveman, throw me over his shoulder and make intense love to me. Above all else, I created an even bigger list of all the qualities I enjoyed about myself. Things I would no longer compromise like my dignity, self-love, and self-worth. Attributes like my authenticity, joy, commitment, wisdom, honor, loyalty and beauty. The list went on and on. I smiled to myself in that prison cell and took a long deep breath.

I was finally happy. Only this time it had nothing to do with Ray or anyone else. I had a golden lasso wrapped around my heart.

I realized we couldn't control the choices other people made and they can't control ours either, unless we allow them to. Regardless of whether or not some people choose to stay together, hold on or let go, it shouldn't shake your spirit no matter what.

The moment I let all that crap go, I looked up and there was that prison guard again.

"Hey, it looks like you'll be released soon, your sister is here to bail you out." he said enthusiastically. As he walked me out he looked at me with his piercing hazel-green eyes and I felt giddy for the first time in years. There was something peaceful and compassionate about him. In a way, he reminded me of my dad. He had been there all along. For the first time in days, I just shut up.

I didn't make it to my wedding that day. As I suspected, Ray and I wanted different things. And even though he didn't want to let me go, he admitted he wasn't ready to get married either. We parted ways peacefully and remained friends. Instead of walking down the aisle, I made a vow to value myself under any circumstance no matter the outcome. Maybe then the real man of my dreams would be able to find me, but I wouldn't put my life on hold until he did.

With that promise, *the Curse* was officially broken. I didn't feel like someone or something supernatural was watching me trying to hold me back anymore. As I found out, the dreaded *Curse* was simply my body's way of warning me about something being off about a situation. Like a flashing "proceed with caution" sign—it had a way of forcing me to be alive to my circumstances.

That night I took my wedding dress off and hung it

in the closet. That night, before I fell asleep, I could have sworn I heard the Wonder Woman theme song playing in the background:

All the world is waiting for you
and the power you possess
In your satin tights
fighting for your rights
And the old red white and blue
Wonder Woman!
Wonder Woman!
Wonder Woman!

Epilogue

I had taken up jogging and one afternoon I jogged to the small jail to visit the officer. After all, he was really sweet and even though he gave me his number that day, I never called him.

I decided to stop in and just say hi and it turned out that he was out to lunch. Lucky for me IHOP had a lunch special and was right around the corner. I had a hunch that's where he would be. I walked in and sure enough, there he was, seated at a booth by himself, eating a stack of blueberry pancakes.

I made myself comfortable in the booth. I no longer needed to feel validated, so I didn't try too hard— was just being myself. I took things slow. I wanted something new, a friend. It felt nice to just chill.

"Pancakes for lunch?" I asked flirtatiously.

"Yeah, I have a sweet tooth." he said with a wink.

His name was Oscar Ramirez, but I called him "Officer." He had wavy brown hair, an awesome olive complexion, and chiseled cheeks. He was fit, but not in an obnoxious "lobsterman" sort of way, more like Bruce Lee. Trim and defined. He was thin framed and I often joked that his pants would fit better on me because he was slim.

"Officer" had the kind of silent confidence that made you feel safe. From that day forward, we met for lunch and tried different spots around the neighborhood while getting to know each other. He loved things about me that I didn't even notice about myself, like my ability to see the humor and light in things and my love of art and music. We just clicked as we began to spend more and more time together. It seemed as though we had the same beliefs, so when he pulled out a small travel toothbrush and excused himself to go brush his teeth after our first romantic dinner out, I knew this time that he was the one.

"Officer" was the first person to believe in my talents. He spent real time with my parents, and he was the one I eventually started a family with.

We have been married four years now and I just gave birth to a beautiful and loving baby boy. Like any relationship we've had our ups and downs, but I can honestly say none of that matters when I look into my son's eyes. Somehow I knew that I'd find an everlasting kind of love and surprisingly I found it through my son.

Curse of the Blue Vagina, La Tea Theatre, NYC

NUDE IN NEW YORK

*I*f you're reading this story in hopes of finding out how to score a great one-night stand in New York... put it down. This is a different kind of nude journey and hopefully by the end of it you'll take a little piece of me with you.

My name is Jonisha. I like to see the humor in everything because without that life can be joyless. People always ask, "How'd you get a black girl's name?" I answer "Same way Kim Kardashian got her ass, from my parents." Rumor had it they conceived me while watching an episode of "Soul Train." Since my name could be considered multi-ethnic, I blended in with everyone. Black kids liked me, white kids thought I was cool and even the Asians shared their shrimp dumplings with me. I was a favorite amongst teachers too. "Hey, let me rub your shoulders," Mr. Grover purred. My fifth-grade teacher was such a gross old dude. He made all the little girls sit on his lap.

Except me, I wasn't okay with that, at least not unless he allowed me to snack in class and turn my homework in late.

I'm from the small town of Bridgeport, Connecticut. Growing up, there wasn't much to do in my home town except go to parades. There was a parade for everything. "Thanksgiving Day" parade, "Christmas Day" parade, the "Big Women in Spandex Day" parade, which later came to be known as the major holiday, the "Puerto Rican Day parade." I had lots of relatives in that one. They didn't even use real balloons; they just had my big fat Boriqua cousins hanging out of their windows, lookin' like they were floating in the sky shouting, "Que viva Puerto Rico."

My parents kept to themselves, so we rarely spent the holidays with other family members. But, on those rare occasions that we did, my parents went ballistic preparing. My mother was like a drill sergeant, organizing the manpower available to her. Having guests was more of a hassle than a joy for us. My dad and I, even my 2-year old baby sister, Jennifer, was given chores.

I always found it odd that when family decided they wanted to come over, everyone had to cater to them as if they were guests staying at the Four Seasons. I didn't understand why we couldn't just be ourselves when people came over. If the house wasn't perfect, then so be it. After all these weren't just some strangers visiting, they were our family. What should have mattered most was that we were eating a good meal and laughing together.

All winter long, relatives would stop over to visit

and it drove my Mom nuts. I, on the other hand, was thrilled when they swung by, because it meant my parents would be forced to turn the heat on. Our house was always on the cold side, no matter what season it was. During winter nights, when I'd lay asleep in bed, I didn't even have blankets; just one thin ass sheet that felt more like it was made out of paper towels sewn together.

After my Titi Clara's husband passed away, she'd come spend time with us as often as twice a week. My parents tried to avoid her as much as possible. Until one day, she just popped up unexpectedly with a caravan full of churchgoers.

"Quick, hide!" my dad whispered loudly as he shut off the lights.

"Abre la puerta, I know you're in there," my Titi Clara shouted through the other side of the door. We waited silently in the hallway, like if she was the big bad wolf about to blow our house down. All of a sudden, I had a giggling fit. It was a dead give-away, so dad was forced to open the door.

"Oh, Titi Clara, we had no idea it was you!" he denied.

"Shame on you! I came all the way from New York to see you."

While my aunt scolded my dad, my mother quickly ran upstairs to make my sister and I look more presentable.

"Shit!" she cussed. "Jonisha, get over here. Put on this dress!" she demanded. "Get these stockings on and where are your panties?"

My grandma had gotten me a package of undies that were labeled with each day of the week. I hated them because they were huge and sagged, so I'd rip them off and swap them out for my strawberry shortcake bathing suit bottoms instead. It's not like my parents took us swimming often, besides they were a cuter option. By the time mom finished getting me ready, I looked like a human piñata. I wore bright, feminine dresses with different colored ribbons and bows on the sleeves and chest. In my hair were a bunch of candy-colored matching barrettes. Once dressed, she'd proudly parade me around the room.

Instead of blindfolded people hitting me with a stick, my aunt's friends would sling compliments and praises while squeezing my cheeks. Sometimes they'd even grab my butt cheeks too, and just go on about how cute I was. "Who the hell are these people?" I wondered. Then all of a sudden the adults went from being all sweet to getting all serious about how I needed to be more disciplined. One by one they would chime in and give a list of rules for me to follow. They'd say, "don't do this", or "don't do that." My handicapped Uncle Papo would glare at me with his glass eye and add "Don't stare."

"But that eye doesn't move." I said studying his bad eye.

"Jonisha that is not nice go to your room." my dad said all embarrassed.

My parents were such hypocrites. They used to talk shit about Tio Papo and his glass eye all the time, but if I said something truthful, forget about it. They would gasp, and I'd be the one in trouble.

Just where did Tio Papo get off saying anything to anyone? He had the worst manners of all. He was always farting and interrupting people. And he never followed anyone's rules. In fact, it wasn't until doctors threatened to amputate his leg, that he finally stopped stuffing his face with flan and talking at the same time.

While these people were over our house, I was forced to sit still and listen to boring ass stories that were repeated over and over again. The only goofy tale I liked was the one Titi Clara's sister Esperanza told about the time her husband drew a smiley face on her butt with a marker when she was asleep. The next day when Esperanza went to the doctor's office for a check up, she couldn't understand why both her doctor and his assistant began laughing uncontrollably. It wasn't until she took a shower later that evening and caught a glimpse of her backside in the full-length mirror, that she saw a huge smiley face drawn on her ass.

I watched my family drink cup after cup of coffee feeling helplessly trapped on the couch. So to keep myself entertained, I'd pull pranks. Sometimes, I'd even strip down and run around completely naked. Everyone grew uncomfortable and silent. This made me laugh. There was nothing developed to see. But I was old enough to know better so I got a good smack on the ass and my punishment was being forced to eat *No Frills* cereal for breakfast the next morning. (If there was ever a cereal that tasted like ass, I'm sure this was the one.) I've heard of Capn' Crunch, but who the hell was Pirate Munch?

As Titi Clara got older she visited us in the suburbs less and less. Rumor had it she'd gotten sick and couldn't do as many road trips. It was then that she decided to create the tradition of hosting the holiday parties at her place. This excited my parents because they secretly no longer wanted to hold the Christmas get-togethers at our place. So we headed to NYC for the weekend.

My parents had a clunky, blue Cadillac they thought was fancy. But for me it felt like we were driving around town in a large fishing boat rather than a car. And, it reeked of gas.

As we set off from CT to NYC, I watched the snow-covered treetops transform into skyscrapers. Dad turned on the radio and popped in a Joe Cuba cassette to the song "Can You Feel It?"

I could see the sparkling lights from hundreds of honking cars as they passed us on the highway. Dad was always a slow driver. He followed the rules of the road and didn't seem to mind being flipped off. According to him going 30 mph on the highway, was fast enough. The twinkling lights that engulfed the city mesmerized me. In my neighborhood we had a few street lamps that gave off a dull glow, but this was spectacular.

The city was plastered with tall buildings that were

stacked up like Legos. Unlike Connecticut where the stores in my town were driving distance, little shops and restaurants lined the streets of every block.

When we arrived in my Titi Clara's neighborhood, it was unlike anywhere else I had ever been. People of different ethnicities were walking up and down the block and you could hear the sounds of music blasting from all the different apartment buildings. Titi Clara loved to dance and played her old Spanish *Navidad* tunes the loudest. We walked up six flights of stairs to get to her tiny apartment. Despite the size of the place, she would throw the biggest parties.

Everyone that lived in that apartment building had an open door policy. So neighbors from all over the complex eventually made their way to Titi's big bash. Her place was crawling with people I'd never met, and their kids.

Puerto Rican families rarely hire a babysitter when they go to house parties…Especially during the holidays. After we ate and unwrapped our presents, we'd be stuck in the "coatroom." (A bedroom where the bed would have coats on it piled up so high, you'd have no choice but to sit on the floor.)

There'd also be a big old school television set in this room with about a hundred other kids squished together lying on their stomachs in front of it. All along the top of the TV, and even on the floor next to it, there was an overabundance of different sized elephant figurines staring at us, all with their trunks up for good luck.

In my day, we'd be watching *Eight is Enough* and after three or four episodes, I'd had enough of feeling claustrophobic in this crowded ass room. So once all my little cousins fell asleep right there on top of each other, I was ready to explore.

I snuck out of the room to hang out with the adults who were so drunk they didn't even notice I was lurking in the background. I walked through the beaded curtain that separated the living room and the dining room. I scoped out my family as they indulged in more of our famous Puerto Rican delicacies: pernil, (*roasted ham*), arroz con gandules, (*rice with pigeon peas*), Valencia cake (*a famous neighborhood cake*) and lots of Coquito (*a sweet eggnog-like alcoholic drink made with rum, eggs and coconut milk*). By the time I got to my third sip of Coquito, I thought I was drunk.

I glanced over at the three-foot high Christmas tree and saw that everyone including my grandma's pet chicken Pio had an ornament. Pio had been a part of the family for 17 years. Seriously, she lived that long. When she died, my entire family was so devastated, that we held a funeral for her at a local park.

As the adults opened up their gifts, I listened to them gossip using Nuyorican secret code names like "Fulano" and "Fulana" *(so-and-so)* to disguise who they were talking about. Like, instead of saying, "Uncle Hector is an alcoholic," they'd say, "Fulano drank two bottles of Jack Daniels before his job interview. Que Estupido."

Everyone was having so much fun. They kicked off their shoes and started dancing. I grabbed a pair of socks that were on the floor and finally let my presence be known by putting on a show starring "Fulano and Fulana," except in my show I used real names.

"Hi, I'm Julio. My idea of lifting weights is carrying two buckets of KFC up the stairs."

"Hi, Jose. I'm Daisy! All I want for Christmas is a brush for the hair under my arms."

Suddenly, the room fell silent. I had single-handedly quieted a room full of Puerto Ricans. I didn't think anybody had been listening. And just when I thought I was gonna get the beating of my life, I could hear some chuckles escaping my relative's mouths.

Thank God for liquor. My Titi Clara, the only sober one, came over to me. "You know, Jonisha, when I make café con leche, I have to have all the right ingredients. If it's too hot people don't drink it, if it's too cold they spit it out. But a good cup of coffee is made with love. So next time you do little show, add some love."

Then she handed me a teeny cup of coffee. It was yummy! I looked out the window and noticed people were still walking around outside after midnight, listening to their boom boxes and laughing. In my hometown, if you saw someone outside after eleven it meant they were either homeless or a spouse had thrown them out for cheating. Something about being in this city made me feel like I could be myself. As I looked around me, somewhere between my family's wild laughter and my grandpa throwing up on the rug, I decided, "When I grow up, I'm moving to New York City."

*A*fter attending college in Connecticut, I ended up transferring to a small theatrical conservatory in New York City. I hadn't really planned on becoming an actress, I just loved the classes and considered teaching or maybe directing someday. I was good at it and used my talents in school as an excuse to finally make my dream of living in the city come true. My aunt still resided in her small apartment in Brooklyn and she had agreed to let me stay with her until I could get my own place.

I'll never forget my first week in the city. I was totally lost. The streets were teeming with people who seemed like different colonies of ants, focused to get to their destinations. It was hard for me to keep from getting knocked over because I didn't have the velocity of a New Yorker, yet. I was a dawdler in that I took pleasure in the world around me and wasn't rushing like a speed walker.

As I walked around Manhattan studying my subway map, I looked up and noticed that there were men everywhere, young, old, cute, funny looking, fat, metro, homo and hetero. At this point in my life, I had only had one boyfriend in high school and had only dated a couple of guys in college. Although getting into a relationship and meeting men in this city was not my focus, I was enjoying their appreciation of me. Every corner I turned there were guys blowing kisses, hooting, hissing, shouting praises and making comments like:

"God bless you sweetheart."

"Hey Precious, what's your number?"

"I love you!"

"Move it!"

"Get the fuck out of the way!"

I had written down the subway directions to get to Titi's on a post-it sticky. I wondered if she would be even more fun now that I was all grown up.

"This is the D Train to Coney Island. Next stop 34th street," said the subway conductor over the PA system.

I had never actually been on a subway before. It was awesome, almost like I had front-row tickets to a theatre at every stop we made. These subway performers were Broadway's rejects that possessed major talent despite their shortcomings. Within an hour, I had seen a blind guitar player, a deaf singer and footless tap dancer.

I began to get restless. It seemed like it was taking forever to reach my station. Finally, we made another stop and I was able to nab a seat for myself as more people piled into the car. Over the scratchy intercom, the conductor yelled, "Stand clear of the closing doors, please."

As the doors closed, a small African-American man wearing a brown suit and matching hat walked to the center of the car and opened up his bible.

"Excuse me, ladies and gentlemen on this fine lovely day! I have a message for you... You are all going to HELL! But the Good Lord, Jesus Christ, came to me in a dream and said if you all just give me two dollars each, YOU can all be saved." he preached.

I had given away all of my loose change to different performers and had nothing left. This did not make him happy.

"The Good Lord don't like cheap," He frowned. As people ignored him, I struggled to find two dollars to save my soul. He pointed for me to check my other pocket but no luck. All I had was two buttons and some gum wrappers.

"Just gimme $2," he begged.

I sat there and pretended to doze off, when he was immediately pushed aside by a Chinese man with a bag full of trinkets.

"One dolla battery, two dolla yo-yo, three dolla box of maxi pads... with wings!"

He stood right in front of me and leaned forward.

"For a dolla fifty you get a date with me and free delivery of shrimp fried rice," he teased.

As the preacher continued to demand his two dollars from me, the Chinese man shoved a box of maxi pads in my face. "Only one dolla, a good deal for you."

"That won't clean up the blood of Jesus sacrificed for us," the preacher interjected.

I couldn't escape these guys and to make matters worse I was squished between a screaming child and "Rico Suave," who leaned in and whispered Spanglish nothings in my ear.

"Muy bonita. Te amo. Gimme a kiss." I slowly inched away from Rico Suave.

"Look sir, I'm just trying to get downtown. Can you move over a bit? Thanks." I was seriously getting annoyed.

Then, all hell broke loose. At the next stop, the little kid next to me hopped off his seat, ran toward the doors and began kicking at them repeatedly to keep the doors from closing. His mother did nothing to stop him. As the doors would keep from closing, it would ring and set off some sort of alarm. The conductor hopped on the loudspeaker and screamed, "Please stop playing with the damn doors!"

"No, don't do that," I said nicely to the kid as I tried to get his mother's attention so she could pull the little bastard away.

The preacher saw I was distracted and raised his voice. "Now, you gotta gimme five dollars to be saved," he barked.

What was wrong with this guy, couldn't he bother someone else? Rico Suave put his arm around me. "Mira mami, let me lick you?"

"What? Will you get your tongue out of my ear?" I felt like I was Little Red Riding Hood and they were all different versions of the Big Bad Wolf.

"Leave me alone, I'm just trying to get to my aunt's house!" I cried.

I shoved the guy away from me and bumped into the little boy. He started crying. "Mommy, she hit me!" His mother pushed up against me and said,

"Oh no you didn't, I'll beat yo' ass."

"I didn't hit him!" I couldn't believe this shit was happening to me.

Just then, the preacher, the Chinese man, and everyone else seemed to talk at the same time and it just escalated.

"Donate, you sinning bitch!"

"Let me just touch your legs."

"Mommy, she pushed me!"

Finally, I stood up and yelled. "Shut the fuck up! Would you all just shut the fuck up?"

After my outburst, everyone shut up. Suddenly the train made an emergency stop.

As we pulled to a screeching halt, the conductor hopped on the PA system and said, "Because the doors are now officially broken, you all have to get out and walk to your final destination."

By the time I arrived at Titi Clara's door, I was exhausted and just wanted to get to sleep. Her apartment was exactly the same way it was when I was kid, with the exception of the invasion of new elephant figurines. More than she had when I was a kid. They weren't just lining the TV anymore, now they were everywhere, the kitchen, and she even had a few on top of the toilet too.

"Eat something, you look hungry. Here take a plate," she insisted.

"No thanks Titi Clara. Maybe later." I sweetly declined.

"Then have some café." she persisted.

"Um, not right now, I'm so tired." I insisted.

My aunt had prepared a feast for my arrival and she was determined to make me eat whether I wanted it or not. I heard her words in slow-mo as she pointed out all of the Puerto Rican foods that were spread across the dining table.

"Alcapurrias (*stuffed yucca fritters*), mofongo (*mashed plantains with garlic*) and your favorite tripas, (*cow intestines, yuck!*)."

The more I protested, the more food she put on the table. I finally gave in and had a plate of Mofongo and platanos maduros *(sweet fried plantains.)* That hit the spot, it was so delicious, I had two more servings.

"Tomorrow, I will make rice, beans, and Chuletas. Then we go to church."

I felt like I was ten years old all over again. "Church on a Tuesday?" I whined. The whole point of living with her was so that I could gain some independence, but instead I was reverting backwards. I had to get my own place fast. If not, I'd end up joining the menagerie of elephants begging to escape.

Over the next few months, I got a little more acquainted with city life. I learned how to ride (I mean, survive) the subway, how to hail a cab and dodge my aunt's church dates.

I had come to learn that my Titi Clara had become an avid churchgoer due to the fact that she had beaten cancer and attributed her healing to her strong Christian faith. She went to church every day. And each time she invited me to tag along, I had to create new excuses to keep me from going with her. It wasn't that I didn't believe. It was just that I felt like church was for old people who were trying to get into heaven in their last few days remaining on earth.

After living with my aunt for a couple of weeks, getting my own place became my mission. I started attending the conservatory in the city I was accepted to. Although classes would keep me pretty busy some days,

I wanted to get a part-time job for my off days.

I looked in the paper and dropped off resumés at local stores and cafés. I was hoping to save enough money for my big move. Eventually I signed up with *Rejex Temps* in Manhattan. They quickly placed me on my first assignment at "Whack 'Em", a hip new ad agency. That's when I met Merie. She was not only the owner but an ad executive. Her company was looking for fresh faces to work their front desk. I walked into her office and she smiled tightly and said, "You're late."

I looked at my watch as well as the clock on the wall and couldn't help but notice that her clock was frozen and I was actually on time. I attempted to defend myself.

"Hi, I'm Jonisha. Actually your clock is broken..." She cut me off mid-sentence. "If I had a gun to your head and I told you I would pull the trigger in one minute if you didn't get here on time... would you be here?"

I didn't want to respond. Merie had crazy eyes. She jumped in, "Just answer me, Toshiba."

Getting placed here even temporarily wasn't looking good. She didn't like me, plus she kept screwing up my name and there was no correcting her.

"Jonitza," she started, "you failed the punctuality test. Let's see how you do on our integrity test!"

She then flipped open her folder and broke out a questionnaire and red sharpie.

"If you were hired and you found someone stealing money from the department, what would you do?

A. Tell your boss, B. Tell the person, who took it, to put it back, Or C. Offer not to tell on them and suggest splitting the money."

I was about to answer A, but instead she answered for me.

"My guess is C." She checked off her own answer with the red sharpie and then threw her coffee mug across the room. She was blind with anger and wasn't even talking to me anymore.

"You know why you don't have the answers? Because you don't know anything about me, Mom!"

Turns out she needed a therapist, not an assistant. What a whack job!

In high school, my black friends were the only people who pronounced my name correctly. They also taught me never to be afraid to correct anyone who messed it up. They felt that my name was part of my uniqueness. A trait they insisted I proudly embrace.

My girls always taught me to prize myself, yet there I was at that office acting like this woman's doormat. Needless to say, that job assignment didn't work out.

Eventually, the temp agency placed me with a new up-and-coming web company for a few weeks. I was always good on the phone and had completely forgotten that aside from a paper route, I also used to do quite a bit of telemarketing after high school. I looked forward to doing sales for this new business. I knew I would be great at it. Over the phone sales was my thing. I was called in to meet the boss, Steve, to start work with him one-on-one on Columbus Day.

I didn't have any plans so I came in and set up shop. Steve and I made our introductions over the phone and we seemed to hit it off. Then when I met him in person, all of a sudden he became cold toward me. It was weird. I worried I didn't look the part because I don't think I've ever really had a good hair day. Regardless, no one over the phone could see my messy hair or me, so I remained confident in my ability to sell and get the job done.

It's always harder to work when someone is there watching you, hoping to prove their preconceived notions right about who they think you are, but I was up for the task. I wasn't going to make the same mistake I made at the previous job where I allowed myself to become insecure. As far as I was concerned I was there to work, so what he thought of me, was none of my business. So when asked me if I could read in English. I said, "No, I got accepted to Yale and got a scholarship to UCONN for finger-painting." He was such an ass.

He made assumptions about me and my level of intelligence based on my brand of shoes, which at the time were from Fayva. It became clear that the problem wasn't me. He just couldn't admit that the type of employee he was looking for, was a man. I finished off the day gracefully and made at least three sales, (which was my goal for the day.) He was impressed.

In the end he offered to make me a full-time employee based on my performance (and mainly because I'd proven him wrong). I respectfully declined and never went back.

My temp agency was running out of options for me, but finally found an opening at a theatre. There I was at the Promenade Theatre on Broadway dressed as an usher. I began to notice that if you filled up the empty seats in the orchestra section, you got tipped. Week after week I hooked people up with "upgraded" seats regardless of getting tipped. Hell, they were empty anyway and the performers always appreciated a seemingly packed house.

"Your seats for this fab production of *Three Sisters* are way up in the nosebleed section. But go ahead take those two seats in the orchestra section, looks like the ticket holders are a no show," I would say. I thought I was doing a good deed by providing great customer service, until the day I got busted and was released from my duties.

As the stage curtains were rising, I fetched my coat before I could be escorted out. I wanted to avoid the dramatic announcement of me being fired to the rest of the employees.

On some occasions, when I wasn't getting anywhere, I would get messages and nudges from the other side. It was especially important to listen to the universe when shit hit the fan. Signs are there to be picked up on and followed. It's the universe's way of telling you "not that way, this way." But, I had ideas about where my life should be headed and felt the universe was ignoring me.

I finally gave in and attended a church service with Titi Clara. My private prayers needed to be amplified. It was packed and she knew everyone.

"Esmeralda, hi!" she yelled from across the church. "Did you get the birthday card I sent you?"

"Yes, I did, thank you!" she said as she blew her a kiss.

"Lucy, this is my niece," she said to another woman wearing bright yellow palazzo pants with a matching flower printed blouse.

"Oh! This is the one that needs Jesus? Sweetie, if you turn to him, you will have all of your needs met..." she whispered to me.

After a few more introductions, I sat down just as the sermon was about to begin. A few minutes later, I felt a tap on my shoulder.

"Excuse me, young lady, on this fine lovely day. Is this seat taken?" It was that guy from the subway. Luckily he didn't remember me.

Although it was hard to admit, I found the service to be uplifting. The priest spoke about overcoming obstacles by having the kind of faith we did when we initially came forth into this existence as children. He encouraged us to give it a try during the hard times because worrying would only make problems seem bigger than what they are.

That evening after I took a shower, I opened my underwear drawer to find that my thong panties had been replaced with a package of white granny panties and a small photo of Jesus with a prayer written on the back. I was immediately bothered by the invasion of privacy. What if I had a package of condoms in there? Then what? Would my aunt have thrown me out? I took a deep breath and realized she only had the best intentions. I took the photo of Jesus and tucked it under my pillow. Tonight he would be the one to comfort me and take away my frustration.

As time went on, living with my Titi Clara became increasingly difficult, because she wanted me to do everything. Clean the house, buy groceries, answer the phone and take her to her doctor visits. Between school, running errands and working part-time here and there, I barely had any time to myself. I couldn't wait to get away.

I was finally hired to be a full-time stock clerk at a local pharmacy. The problem was, I worked the graveyard shift. In order to stay awake, I had to think of creative ways to keep busy.

"Hey, Mrs. Kumar, I have an idea for how we can boost sales in the feminine hygiene department." I said as I walked her over to the snacks and freezer section.

"Put them in the snack section. You see if the snacks and fem products are sold together, you can kill two birds with one stone and make more money." I was proud of my idea. Usually when I started craving snacks, it meant *aunt flow* was coming to town. She stared at me as if I had two heads.

"Are you crazy? We don't need help boosting sales, we need you to get it together and stock more shelves." She shouted in her thick Hindu accent.

Apparently Mrs. Kumar thought I needed to learn to respect the boundary between food and hygiene products and forbid me from putting the Twinkies and tampons on the same isle.

The store traffic was non-stop. The later it got, the more customers would come in. By three in the morning, I was delirious. The graveyard shift should be outlawed because it makes you go bats. Once Mrs. Kumar went home, I began to stage commercials for incoming customers in the middle of the store desperate to keep myself awake. It was like a theatrical public access version of the Carol Burnett show. Sometimes my sketches would be in Spanglish and I'd have fun with my Mexican co-worker Lucia.

"Mama, tengo problemas aqui," *(Mama, I have problems right here)*. I'd say pointing down to my private parts.

Then she'd join in and say, "Try aisle seven Mijita. If you got an itch, you would need to do more than splash water up there. Use this strawberry scented douche. And, it doesn't sting like soap."

"Wow, there are so many flavors," I said in a goofy character voice.

"Scents, not flavors mijita. This isn't Victoria's Secret. They're not making this for your man." We had a blast together goofing around but generally our late night customers were not amused. That is until Leo strolled in to shop at 4am with his tiny girlfriend. He loved my sense of humor and laughed at all my silly jokes. I came to find out that Leo was a hack talent manager that owned a talent management company called Double D's. (Dwarfs with Big boobs.) When I finally convinced myself I wasn't going to fit that agency, we became friends. He sashayed to the counter with his hot, small girlfriend, Peep, in one arm and a package of condoms in the other.

"Why don't you try to work on the stage?" he suggested in his thick Jersey Shore Italian accent.

"No thanks, Leo, I'm not interested in stripping." I replied.

"Not that stage, fool. A stage in a theatre." He laughed as he handed me a *Backstage* newspaper. I had seen this paper circulating at my school. At that time, however, students weren't allowed to audition or pursue acting until we all at least graduated.

I gladly accepted the paper from Leo, just to take a peek. After all, I reasoned that if I was gonna work a job, it might as well be one I had fun doing.

Later that afternoon when I finally crawled out of bed, Titi Clara served me a cup of her famous Bustelo espresso with warm milk as I looked through the *Backstage* weekly. On every page, it seemed like there were openings for everything, from theatre productions, to films, and even a few TV commercials.

I decided to audition for my next job. Besides, I'd already learned some auditioning techniques in school, how hard could it be in real life?

I became inspired. Up to this point, my only dream was to become a New Yorker. Maybe it was time to venture out and take a crack at a bigger dream.

As I refilled my cup of coffee, I saw an ad for a gig that paid five hundred bucks for a weekend performance of the show called *Five Women Wearing the Same Dress*, in the Hamptons. The play was about five bridesmaids getting to know each other after their friend gets married.

The next day, I sat in the lobby waiting to audition, for the first time in my life. I was nervous. Although I'd gone through a similar process to get into my conservatory's dramatic program, for some reason that hadn't scared me. I buried myself in my sides and feverishly tried to learn my lines for the character of Mindy, when Kerri walked in. She had played a couple of small supporting roles on Broadway. She knew everyone in the room.

"Yo! Sharon, Jennifer and Shaniqua! Guess who had four lines in *Sex and the City*? That's right. ME! Kerri, with a hard K!"

Her and her friends high-fived each other and squealed as they huddled together to swap audition stories. Once a couple of her chums left, she turned to me.

"Who are you? I've never seen you around here before. What agency are you with? C+Talent?" she asked with that condescending smile that made me believe for a second that she was actually being sincere.

"I don't belong to an agency. I found an ad for the audition in the paper," I replied.

She was absolutely horrified and quickly changed the subject.

"What perfume are you wearing?" she sneered. Before I could answer, she faked a sneeze. "Achoo! It's giving me allergies!"

I glanced at the clock on the wall hoping to be called into the room next. She hopped up to the sign-in table and glanced at the clipboard.

"I'm almost up!" she said adjusting her boobs.

"They call 'em boob jobs, cause first you get the boobs and then you get a job. So I'm booking this today!" she announced.

"Do you have them? Or are you just one of those healthy girls?" she winked as if she were suggesting I were big.

This chick was a firecracker who was going to light everyone up one-way or the other. I seriously considered smacking the shit out of her, but I kept it cool. After all, I wasn't there for her and she wasn't gonna scare me away.

"Where'd you get your outfit? Conway's?" she said going for the jugular.

Conway's is like the Payless Shoes version of clothing. I shopped there all the time, but fuck her. She kept dissing everyone around her, and we all just ignored her. She obviously wasn't a real New Yorker, because if she were she wouldn't be so disrespectful of me or of the melting pot that this city was known for.

"Can you keep it down out here?" reprimanded the hall monitor. "You're a distraction. These walls are paper thin and the people inside that room can hear everything."

"Oh, I'm so sorry," she said as she pointed at me. "I think she's at the wrong audition. I was just trying to let her know."

When she said that, I looked around and noticed that I didn't see any other brunettes waiting in the lobby. Even Shaniqua, the black girl sitting next to me, was blonde.

As I gathered my belongings, Kerri suddenly became very helpful. "Listen, I'm sorry. I'm really competitive. When I was a kid Mom forced me to be in beauty pageants and I guess that's where it all began. Anyway, they have this hidden camera show they're auditioning for in Harlem. You have to go in and do something outrageous. But remember, it's set up like a hidden camera show, so be natural."

She scribbled something on a piece of paper and handed me it to me. It was an address with some directions. "Good luck," she said as she flashed me another one of her phony ass smiles. I didn't trust her at all, but I was desperate for a job and forced myself to believe she was sincere about the audition. As I was leaving, I went to cross my name off the list... and I noticed her last name was Gonzalez. What a hater.

I took the subway to Harlem and followed the directions, which led me to a small Soul Food restaurant, *Jermayne's Jerk Chicken 'n Greens.* There was a mirror behind the cashier and I assumed it was a two-way mirror. Without hesitating, I jumped on the counter top and began to sing the McDonald's jingle because it was the only food jingle I knew.

> *Would you like a Big Mac,*
> *McDLT, a Quarter Pounder with some cheese,*
> *Filet o' Fish?*
> *A Hamburger, a Cheeseburger, a Happy Meal?*
> *McNuggets, tasty golden French fries, regular*
> *and larger sizes!*

I waited for the camera crew to bust out from the back room and say, "You're hilarious. You're hired!" But as I took a closer look, there were no other singing waitresses or a camera crew. The waitress walked away from me, expressionless.

I quickly hopped off the table and shot out of there like a bullet, I was so embarrassed.

*S*everal months had passed and I became discouraged about living in New York. I wondered if I'd actually join the competitive world of the arts once I graduated school. I just wasn't cut out for that cutthroat type of career. I had no clear goal and still no new job. Apparently everyone in my aunt's complex found out. It seemed like lately the neighbors knew the outcome of my days before I did. It was as if Titi Clara leaned out of her window with a bullhorn and yelled, "Listen everybody, Jonisha still hasn't found a job!"

As soon as I arrived at the building, our neighbors leaned out of their windows and offered suggestions.

Jennifer was the first to console me. "Shit happens you know. It's all good. Hey if you want, you could always walk my dog for a few bucks."

"Um, no thanks" I declined after her dog started growling and snapping at me.

"I need a window washer," shouted John from the fifth floor.

"Why don't you go to church with your aunt more often?" inquired Juanita.

As I was making my way upstairs, one of the neighbors who I had never seen before pulled me to the side. "Psst, you should see my cousin la espiritista! Her name is Dona Luz, she can get rid of the demons that are holding you back." she warned.

She handed me a small business card with her cousin's name and number and then disappeared behind the dark apartment door. I tucked the card into my pocket, rolled my eyes and sat on the steps to drink the rest of my Malta soft drink in peace.

I had gone from being hopeful to hopeless. It had been months since I had visited my parents back in CT and longed for that peaceful silence I once called absolute boredom. I also started to feel like I had overstayed my welcome, but didn't really have any other place to go.

Although she didn't say it, I could feel the tension building between Titi Clara and me, but I was stuck and I couldn't turn back and go home now. To ease the pressure, I decided to start pitching in and paying whatever I could toward rent even though she never asked me to. This way I could stay a little longer, only problem was that with my new rent bill, I'd barely be able to save enough money. Would I ever be on my own?

I lay in bed that night staring at the cracks in the ceiling. I began to meditate on how to simplify my dream of living on my own in the Big Apple. I loved performing and writing but could I realistically make a living doing this? And if not, what else was out there for me? I questioned if I'd ever meet the man of my dreams here. I wondered when I would get married and have a family of my own. Just then the sounds of my aunt's footsteps approached my door and interrupted my thoughts. I rarely shut the light off in my room because of the warm glow it gave off. So every night before she'd go to sleep my aunt would stop at my door on her way to her room and say in Spanish, "Apaga la Luz. Te Quiero" (*Shut off the light. I love you.*)

As I was about to turn out the light and get some sleep, my Tia came into my room and invited me to have coffee with her. I was tired but got up and sat with her at the table.

"It will all work out, mija," she said sweetly. "Look at me. I had cancer and if that went away, anything is possible."

She smiled and handed me a cup of Joe, which only kept me up thinking the rest of the night.

Later that week, I had gotten another temp assignment at the Twin Towers. I worked on the 96th floor. I was a mail delivery girl at a bank for a few weeks. As I went to different floors to pick up mail, I'd always stop to look out the windows. It was such a special experience working in a bustling, important place. But, I never took the time to check out the ultimate view from the observatory deck. I'd say, "tomorrow." I figured it would always be there. And sadly, now those beloved towers are long gone.

Although I was offered a position to become permanent at that bank, something inside told me not to take the job. After all, I was still young and not finished with school. Besides it was a long way from my aunt's house and school and my temp agency had promised me other opportunities. It's kind of scary when I think about how I would have been there when those towers went down had I not followed my intuition to leave when I did. I thank God every night for sparing my life and pray for those who didn't make it home on the day the towers went down.

It's funny how when you're a New Yorker, oftentimes you don't make time to visit the sights that make the Big Apple famous: The Statue of Liberty, The Empire State building, Little Italy etc. Unless I was passing them by on the subway, I didn't feel the need to go. I figured I would see these tourist attractions eventually, and never did.

I decided it was time for me to enjoy myself a little since that was the main reason for my moving here to the city. Dancing was one of my favorite things to do. I put on the coolest outfit I could find in my closet and headed out to the club with my classmate Ramon. Ramon and I had scene-study classes together and I had a crush on him. He weighed about 300 pounds and dressed like he weighed 150. He had such a superstar personality and was loads of fun to be around.

We met up in Manhattan, where the nightlife was hopping. The busy streets seemed to be more crowded at night than they did during the day. We decided to go to the Palladium, where the line to get in wrapped down the block, around the corner, and across the street.

A girl in a sparkly bra top and leather pants walked by. Ramon looked me up and down in disappointment, "Betty Boop t-shirt and denim skirt, hot!" he said sarcastically.

Clubs in Connecticut typically closed at 2am with most people leaving by 11pm. But here clubs opened at midnight and stayed open until at least 10am the next day! Some of them even served breakfast.

Because the bouncer letting people in at the club didn't approve of my outfit, he made us go to the back of the line and by the time we got to the front of the door, I was already sleepy. But, it was worth it. Here at these clubs, the music that you heard was not played on the radio. Most of it was either underground mixes or new artists on the verge of stardom. The way the DJ mixed music together, you only had one choice, dance like your life depended on it. At the club, it felt like everyone got along because the music brought us together.

Midway through the night I lost Ramon. It was dark and crowded. At one point all I could see were flashing strobe lights. After hours of hanging at the bar drinking rum and cokes, and dancing alone, I could no longer hold in my pee. As I threaded through the sweaty crowd to the bathroom in the back, I squeezed my legs together tightly to make sure I didn't go on myself. I slithered like a supermodel, my steps twining in and out as I walked in a wobbly line. Luckily, when I passed through the tunnel of ass grabbers, they didn't strike until I made my way back.

When I came back out, a little more sober and clear-headed, it was like I'd developed a sixth sense. Somehow I knew which borough men were from, simply by where they hung out at in the club. Guys from Brooklyn were hanging by the speakers, "Yo this beat is dope son, what?" Guys from the Bronx were in the middle of the dance floor battling it out, "Go Robbie, Go Robbie, keep spinning." And the mama's boys from Queens were by the bar getting chewed out by their girlfriends, "Where were you Johnny, huh? Were you in the bathroom, flirting with girls? Or screwing whores in the corner? My guess is screwing around with whores, you cheating bastard!"

Just then Johnny's girlfriend pulled out a gun and shot it in the air. In an instant, the club was shut down.

I had given up on looking for Ramon, when he staggered out of the club drunk, arm and arm with another guy.

"Sweetie, I'll see you in class," he said. "By the way this is Chewy, my cutie."

Before I could borrow a couple of bucks from him for a cab ride home, he disappeared.

After hours, the only cabs that will take you into other boroughs are gypsy cabs. Gypsy cabs are regular cars, usually, Cadillac's. They'll take you anywhere you want to go in the city for fifteen bucks. I hopped into the gypsy car with my driver, Russell Jones, who was a telemarketer by day and became King Candy Kane the filmmaker, at night.

"The name of my movie is called *Hoochie Coochie Mamas*. It's my first movie and we're lookin' for all kinds of chicks for the flick. You can be an actor, a dancer and a waitress... I ain't picky. As long as you a lady, it's okay. Ya dig? What kind of experience do you have?" he asked.

I reached into my purse, searching for money, and all I could find was 50 cents and a half eaten stick of gum. I struggled with how to break the news to Russell, but engaged in conversation to distract him, until we got closer to my aunt's place.

"Um, well, when I was in high school, one summer I use to be a clown for kids' birthday parties and perform magic tricks."

"You don't say? Hell, in my book a trick is a trick, so you just what we lookin' for. You see you gotta go with the flow, like Cheerios. Get with King Candy Kane, I'm sticky but sweet." he said, which made no sense to me at all.

He went on and on about the film industry and how I could do very well in the business. If I could gather up a few more girls, he would cut me in on the deal.

"I create employment opportunities for ladies all the time and you ain't got to worry about getting your check cashed, 'cause you always get cash on the spot." he assured me.

As we got closer to home, I broke the news to him. "Russell, I'm really sorry, I don't have any money. Can I send you a check?"

He pulled over and slammed on the brakes, which made me pee a little bit.

"What? I don't take checks. I expect you to work it off and pay me back."

I had no choice but to pretend I was going to be his number one sales gal.

"Ok, yeah, I can start next week," I promised. I agreed to come work for him and scribbled a fake number on a piece of paper I pulled out of my bag. He smiled and kept driving.

"Don't worry about the cab fare. I get a cut of everything you make as one of my ladies. Plus, we drop you off at the customer's crib and pick you up when you done. Now what job you heard of that provides free car service?"

I nodded and smiled sweetly, looking for a place I could tell him to drop me off. "Oh, here it is. I'm in this building right here."

He pulled and parked. "You live at the post office?" he questioned suspiciously.

"Uh- no. The building on the corner." I said pointing to a random building I saw.

He stared at me from the rear view mirror and muttered out some riddle.

"A lotta guys compromise to materialize the ass for some good money. Tricks aren't for kids, we in the world of adult films now."

I didn't understand his pimp talk. He clarified.

"It means I'll call you next week."

"I live in Queens, I'm visiting my best friend tonight. So you would have to pick me up there," I lied.

"I shoot my films in Queens all the time. We do it low budget style. One location—my bedroom!"

Luckily, I was only about a block away from my real home. As I pretended to walk toward my best friend's building, he yelled out the window, "Welcome to the team. Don't forget to check out my website, www dot become a ho dot com. Become a ho ho ho…! Merry Christmas!"

*B*etween the club incident and the cab ride, I was reminded of how unprotected I was as a person. I felt like I had to put a mask on just to survive. Is it possible that I was wearing a mask even with my aunt?

When I finally made it upstairs to the apartment, I immediately rushed into the bathroom. To me the bathroom was the safest place for me to just be alone. It seems to be the only place where one is free to admit the thoughts that can only come to you when you're slightly drunk. As I dozed off staring at the plastic shower curtains, one by one random thoughts popped into my head like:

I pretend I'm sleeping on the train, so I don't have to give up my seat.

When I use a public bathroom, sometimes if it's empty, I pee in the handicapped stall cause it's bigger.

When my parents cut cable TV, my boyfriend left me.

When I leave a tip for a waiter at a restaurant, I fold the money so it looks like I left more.

Is it possible that the real reason Boricuas celebrate Three Kings Day Jan 6, is because all the sales on gifts come the day after Christmas?

When a dog humps on my leg, I like it. (Gross, just checking to see if you are still with me, sickos.)

More thoughts came to me in my little sanctuary. I thought about how my parents were dreamers who put their ambitions aside to raise my sister and me. Here I was with no kids and no clue. I wondered how in the hell my folks managed to figure things out after having us at such a young age. I even thought about God. How even though I had very little faith as an adult, I still found myself praying to him once in a blue moon. It felt good to set my fears free, even if there really was no man in the sky listening.

I think the first day I lost some of my childish happy-go-lucky pep was when a drunk driver killed my dog, JR. He was an adorable, loving little Shitzu who I felt at a deep level truly understood me. He was sweet, innocent and very smart. My parents trusted him enough let him out to go for walks occasionally unsupervised. Once he'd walk around the block a couple of times, he'd come right back home. I always remembered him scratching on the door or barking to alert us to let him in.

One night I heard a crash followed by what sounded

like someone yelling the word "Help!" And as we all ran to the window, there he was dragging himself from the middle of the street toward our house. He was in pain. He had been hit by a car and in the end was robbed of his life. It was a heartbreaking and traumatic experience that left me doubting God even existed, because although I prayed and prayed for him to recover, he died anyway.

When my parents came home from the vet, they came back without JR. At that time, I couldn't understand why my pleas to God to make sure my little dog got healed, were ignored. My parents tried to console me by saying that JR would always be with me even if I couldn't see him anymore. Kinda like God. When I asked them to prove it to me, they searched for evidence. My dad gave me a warm hug then said,

"I have proof, but you're gonna laugh cause it may sound silly to you." I listened hoping his proof would ease my pain. "Did you know that God spelled backwards is Dog?" I was flabbergasted. "What's that got to do with it?" I complained. "That's a pretty big coincidence don't you think?" I didn't understand, so I felt worse which made me cry harder. Clearly my parents were clueless about the heartache I felt. He went on. "You don't get it now but some day when you are all grown up and having a bad day, or going through a really tough time, you'll see a dog. And when you do, always remember it's a sign there to tell you that you aren't alone. That God is with you."

What he said meant nothing to me back then, but when he offered to take me out for ice cream, I immediately became hopeful and happy again. What is it about ice-cream when you're a kid? It always turned my frowns upside down.

Years after that incident, I still hadn't completely renewed my faith, but I was ready to try again. As I sat on the cold tiles in the bathroom of my aunt's crib, I decided to give prayer one more shot. I closed my eyes and the toilet became my confessional.

"Hi God. Long time no talk. Um, I feel like I'm losing myself and need to know if I'm living in the right place, or if I'm at least on the right path."

As I patiently waited for an answer, I secretly hoped Morgan Freeman would appear to me dressed in white, standing by the tub, ready to guide me in the right direction. Just then my aunt, who I thought was asleep, interrupted me.

"Jonisha, you awake?" she called. I wanted so badly for her to go back to sleep but it was too late, I could already smell the coffee. I entered the kitchen and the aroma of her sweet-smelling café con leche was enough to cheer me up. It seemed that when I wanted my solitude the most, there she was, Titi Clara standing in the kitchen with a cup of love in her hand. How could I resist?

I never understood how my aunt, who lost the love of her life to cancer, and battled a few health scares herself, had any faith in God at all. When I asked her, she shared that losing the love of her life created a void in her heart that she could only fill with her faith. She said it wasn't easy to believe at first because of all the pain she felt due to her circumstances. But that after a while, she began to feel the presence of God with her all the time. Titi Clara said she began to experience it most not when she was at church, but when she was simply alone at home peacefully sipping her coffee while sitting at the kitchen table. She believed people should stop worrying and be still so that they too can feel the presence of love fill them from the inside out. Hearing her say this in her broken English inspired me.

The holidays were fast approaching and despite the fact that Titi Clara was in good spirits, I noticed things gradually changing. She was once involved in everything, from politics to bingo nights at the church, and now things seemed to have slowed down for her dramatically. She went from dressing sharp and going here and there, to wearing house dresses and hanging out at home. I also noticed her typical bright smile had turned into a worrisome frown.

It seemed like her life was withering before me. Even her energy was different. She was limiting herself to an even smaller world and pushing out the people she once welcomed. I was worried she might ask me to leave, too.

On the day my aunt turned seventy-five, she was as excited as a sixteen-year-old who passed her driving test. I, on the other hand, had woken up in a bad mood. My financial situation was starting to bother me. Not only was I unable to afford a ticket to see Chicago on Broadway that night with my schoolmates, but I was ashamed that I couldn't even come up with ten bucks to buy my aunt a small birthday gift. I grumpily sat at the kitchen table.

I studied the small wrinkles on Titi Clara's face. She was very pretty. Then, Titi opened up a drawer by the stove, pulled out a gift with a red ribbon tied around it and handed it to me. I was touched that here it was her birthday and Titi Clara was giving me a gift.

"For me? Why?" I took it from her enthusiastically and opened it. "It's an old sock." I laughed.

"No, it's el colador. It's the secret to my best café.

Now pay attention. Así que usted puede aprender, (*so you can learn*)." She grabbed a small pot sitting on top o f the stove and filled it with water. After she turned on the burner, she rinsed the colador in the sink under cold running water and turned it inside out.

"At first when you use el colador your café may taste bitter, but then after a while you will learn to make a perfect cup every time." She scooped out a spoon full of some ground espresso beans from a bag of Bustelo she pulled from the cabinet and then sprinkled it into the pot of boiling water. She closed her eyes as if in silent meditation, then placed her hand above the pot. Before shutting off the stove and removing the pot, she smiled and said a little prayer.

"Gracias a Jesucristo para todo en mi vida." Then she took the colador and poured the contents of the pot into it as she held it above a coffee mug. She added some warm milk that was already prepared, 3 spoonfuls of sugar and handed it to me. YUM! It was her best tasting cup yet. I was impressed.

Her eyes lit up as she shared a bit more of the history behind this reusable coffee sock.

"This colador has been in our familia for generations. My great grandmother gave it to my grandmother, who gave it my mother, who gave it to me. Every time you use it, think only of love, and the café you make will always taste good."

I gave her a hug. She squeezed me tightly then said,

"Always remember that love is my secret ingredient." She meant well. I knew this lesson was coming from her heart.

"Happy Birthday Titi." I'm sorry I don't have anything for you…"

"Don't worry about that." she said cutting me off. "Just make me café con leche someday."

I smiled and then stared at the colador. It looked like those little booties you try on at a shoe store, which is then attached to a small wooden stick. It was stained and shriveled. It resembled a dripping doo-rag.

Although it was a very sweet gift, part of me also found it slightly embarrassing that the colador was considered a family heirloom that was now being passed down to me. Never the less, it was indeed a special treasure. I tucked it safely in my night drawer next before going to sleep.

*O*ne snowy winter morning, after a few weeks had passed, my frustration about not living on my own began to build. As I looked out the window and saw snow falling, I realized it meant only one thing. That I'd be stuck in the apartment with my aunt, forced to listen to her repeat the same stories of her life over and over again.

Titi Clara had a rich life before she started staying in. She had a great sense of humor, knew lots of people, and was a wonderful storyteller. But lately, nothing she said surprised or touched me. I had become too familiar with the ins and outs of her stories and daily routines. I knew how she would look when she stepped out of her bedroom, and how many cups of coffee she would have throughout the day. And I also knew she would rely on a combination of religion and a passive acceptance of life to embrace whatever might come her way. I was over it.

A few weeks later I was thrilled when I got hired to work as a clown for a kid's birthday party. Finally, I was able to get away.

I stepped into a decorated roller rink dressed in my costume complete with full-face makeup and a bright red clown nose. I was pretty happy to be at this party. "Hey kids, it's Clowny the Clown." I shouted gleefully. The children were not pleased to see me at all. A couple of them even cried. Why is it that most kids hate clowns? We aren't all creepy. Anyway, they chased me around and tormented me the whole time I was there.

"Kids, kids! Take a seat," I said in my squeaky clown voice to calm them down. "No, no! This is my real hair; don't try to pull it off! Ok, ok! So who wants to see a magic trick?"

When the kids realized they couldn't get any part of my costume off, they stopped tugging at me and chased each other around in skates.

"Can you just sit down for a few minutes? The magic show is very short, I promise." I pleaded. I spent hours the night before preparing the little magic show I had in store for the kids, but these little fuckers ignored me.

The only attention I seemed to get was from the parents, who formed a circle around me for the purpose of hounding me with their requests:

"Hey, Clown, can you jump around while you juggle?"

"Can we get another picture with you?" "Do you have any other magic tricks?" The birthday boy skated toward his classmates and pushed everyone down who was in his way.

His mom was saying, "Danny's just a little hyper. Danny stop that! Danny please that's not very nice, say you're sorry... Danny no! Danny, come say hi to Clowny!" Finally, the monster stopped bashing his guests, and turned towards me.

Everywhere I went, he followed, poking and hitting me. His mom turned away and he quickly snatched a loose roller skate from the floor, which he threw at me.

"Ouchhhh!" I winced as I rubbed my head.

"Shut up, bitch! I can do whatever the hell I want! It's my birthday!"

At this point, I wanted to collect my paycheck. No one would really notice if I snuck away.

But, little Danny grabbed a pen out of his mother's purse and charged at me. I yanked it out of his hand and snapped. I don't know what came over me, but I'm pretty sure it had something to do with the new blue thumbtack sticking out of my ass.

"Listen you evil bastard, calm the fuck down!" I exploded.

Once again, just like when I was a kid, I had managed to single-handedly quiet a room roller rink full of kids and their Jewish parents. His grandparents were the only ones that nodded in approval. Danny ran away upset.

Back at home before I could enter my room, my aunt

stopped and gave me a hug.

"Ay bendito, pobrecita." Oh no, the dreaded 'Ay Bendito', the Puertorriqueños anthem that really means, "You poor sad, pathetic thing!"

The last thing I wanted was anyone feeling sorry for me. I don't know how she knew, but I blame the Nuyorican grapevine. The dude at the concession stand at the roller rink, who lived in our building, must have ratted me out.

After her fifth 'ay bendito' in a row, I felt ashamed so I gently pulled away from her and just nodded. I wanted to be left alone.

Titi Clara told me one of the neighbors was throwing a party for her 6 year-old and suggested I go dressed as "La Cucaracha Martina". She claimed once they saw me I'd get hired. Was she crazy? Another party was the last thing I wanted to do. Especially dressed as a cockroach. (White people have Mickey Mouse. Latinos have La Cucaracha fucking Martina.) I rolled my eyes, walked passed her and went to my room.

My aunt came in soon after and handed me the phone. "Jonisha, it's me, Mommy. I heard all about it… maybe it's time for you to come back home." I hung up the phone and fell asleep.

I wasn't about to give up after one lousy job. I just needed to be disciplined and find a sense of purpose. So I decided to start working out. School had ended and with the extra time on my hands, I took up running in Central Park. My legs got tauter and I had a little less jiggle. I felt good about myself. Then something horrible happened.

One morning after about six weeks of running peacefully through the park, two men came at me from out of nowhere with their guns drawn. I was terrified. I had no cell phone on me at the time. I froze. There was no one there to help me.

During moments like these, you feel helpless. In an instant, my life flashed before my eyes. I assumed they were gonna pull me into the woods to rape and then kill me. I thought about how since I'd moved to New York, I hadn't really spent much time with my parents. I feared that had I gotten murdered, the worst part would be how devastated they'd be when they got the news. Luckily, the robbers just demanded I give them money. I quickly handed them all that I had and they split. I then took off and ran as fast as I could in the other direction. I worried they'd turn around and come after me once they realized I only gave them five bucks.

When I got back home, I locked myself in the bathroom and cried. I was shaken up by the incident and my mind flooded with memories of me not standing up for myself in the past. Here I was in the middle of a crowded city and no one was there to help me, not even myself. I decided it was time for me to become the stereotypical tough New Yorker I'd been avoiding. That meant becoming more vocal. Although I may have stood up to a bully or two when I was a kid, as an adult, I spent time avoiding drama and confrontation. Not anymore. I became determined to not only fend for myself, but also tell it like it is.

*S*hortly thereafter I found myself at an empowerment seminar for women called B.A.B, (an acronym for Become a Bitch), held in the boardroom of a Marriott hotel.

The speaker was a short, skinny, English woman named Emma Powers. She wore small, red-framed glasses, and a green blazer. She spoke into the mic in the center of the room. Emma was surprisingly charismatic.

"My dear ladies, are you tired of people pushing you around? Sick of letting yourselves down and selling yourselves short? Are you answering 'yes,' when you mean 'no?' Then my dear ladies, it's time to value yourselves once and for all!"

There was polite ladylike applause in the audience, and I could hear a couple of "whup, whups."

"Say hello to Jonisha, our newest member of the group." She pronounced my name with an extended emphasis on the "ni." It sounded glamorous.

I pulled out my "Become a Bitch" notebook to scribble down notes. A short-haired Italian woman with a muscle shirt and thick Brooklyn Italian accent stepped on stage to the song Born to be Wild.

"Hey, douchebags! I'm Joe-Ann. The day I became an empowered bitch, I was standing in a long line at Dunkin Donuts while them cashiers were carryin' on a conversation and not helping anybody. I got pissed, right? So I walked to the front of the line, grabbed her by the throat, and said, 'Listen, douchebag, gimme a large coffee and a glazed donut now, or I'll kick your ass!'" The crowd chuckled. "That was just day one of applying Emma's technique! I have been doin' it ever since. My life has completely changed." She flexed her muscles triumphantly.

The ladies toasted her with coffee mugs in the air. Olga was next to take the stage. She wore a slinky black dress with lumpy cleavage hanging out of it. She spoke with a thick Russian accent and her words sounded just as lumpy.

"I am Olga. I use to be a slave to men, like Cinderella. Fuck that Cinderella. Now, I am like Snow White, but so far I have met not the 7 dwarfs, but the 7 dicks: sleazy, spooky, cheapo, creepo, nympho, loco, and yoyo, he was uncircumcised. I already have bags under my eyes; I don't need to see another one around his penis, unless I'm going to the movies and need somewhere to store my snacks. I like sex and I say, be a man about it. And if this is bitchy, then I am a bitch."

Woman after woman took the stage to share stories about how becoming a "Queen Bee", or a "Bitch", impacted them in powerful ways. I admit I was inspired, but could I live up to it? If you were to ask anyone in my family they would say that I didn't need this seminar because according to them, I was a bitch. But for me that just didn't ring true. I was honest yes, but to be a true diva of bitchdom, you have to call people out on their shit without caring about hurting anyone's feelings. As honest as I could be, there were times I shut the fuck up, after all I had a heart.

Next, Leticia from the Bronx danced her way up to the stage and took the mic from the stand. "I been with Cheetoh for two months and I knew something was up when he sent me a Valentines Day card two weeks late, made out of printer paper. At first I was nice and I said 'Thank you.' But then he tried that shit on my birthday and Christmas." The group let out a collective groan. "And it turned out, as I suspected, he'd been spending his money buyin' gifts for some other ho!" The crowd gasped in disbelief. I said, "Hell to the no! He was livin' in my house rent free! I don't think so! So, I ran that mutha fucka over with my car. I'm the queen bee, if you don't serve me, you die!" Queen Latifah's song "Latifah's had it up 2 here" blasted over the loudspeaker. The crowd went berserk and started jumping up and down on their seats.

So much went through my mind as I watched and listened to these women. I began to write down a list of the things that I hated in my life. I started with small things that bugged me like, giving courtesy laughs at someone's unfunny jokes. Then it escalated and I wrote more things down—things like:

I hate lying so people feel more comfortable.

I hate that I still live with my aunt.

I hate that I show only one side of myself to the world, hiding the best part to keep from getting hurt.

I hate when people make false assumptions about me. They seem to catch me on an off day and end up feeling validated by their false beliefs.

I hate being misunderstood

I hate those bastards that held me up.

Why prey on innocent people? Assholes!

Get a fucking job or three if you have too.

The list snowballed and before I knew it, I had filled up four pages of things I had hated.

As Leticia danced her way off the stage, Emma nodded, and it was my turn to speak. "Let it out, girl!" Leticia encouraged. I felt the room grow silent as I took the mic. I was drenched in sweat. What happened to my old self? I saw Joe-Ann in the back of the room roll her eyes. Something in me went off like a time bomb.

"Don't judge me! Who the hell are you to criticize me,

when you don't have your own shit together?" Everyone looked stunned as I proceeded to stand on my chair and keep going. I started to see the faces of the participants transform into the faces of people in my life: family, friends, ex-friends and ex-lovers, even of myself. Moments in my life that I had never dealt with began to pop up. I shouted out things I should have said to anyone in the past that pissed me off.

"Shut up!

Leave me alone. Don't touch me! Stop lying!

Don't touch my French fries!

NO MORE FUCKING COFFEE TITI CLARA!"

After my outburst, I felt dizzy and clear. Everyone in the room was silent. All you could hear was a fan blowing.

A tear rolled down my cheek. I had my breakthrough. There was nothing left to say. All of a sudden the ladies all rose to their feet and erupted in cheers. Finally Joe-Ann, my harshest critic, came over to me and handed me her last glaze donut from Dunkin Donuts.

With my newfound attitude, I was ready for anything. And my first test was to get a damn seat on the train. I hopped on the 6 train during rush hour after class, and it was as if a starting gun went off in my head and the theme song from *Chariots of Fire* was playing in the background. Several of us pushed our way toward the one last seat in the back of the subway car. A man with a business suit whacked me away with his newspaper and tried to squeeze past me. I kicked him in the calf and he fell to the floor. I was halfway there. Next, a woman with a cup of hot tea in hand raced me. She overestimated her athleticism and spilled her scorching tea all over the man with the newspaper. I won! I sat down proud, proud, and proud.

As people shuffled through the doors to leave, one elderly man staggered in and bumped into a teenage boy carrying a boom box.

"Dag you stupid old man, watch where you're going. Loser." he said rudely.

My ancestors come from the beautiful *Isla del Encanto*, aka Puerto Rico, and whenever I see people from our homeland mocked, it immediately tugs on my heartstrings, because my people will just take it.

The old Puerto Rican man pulled out his beer and gave it a kiss. He spoke directly to me in Spanglish. "Aqui conmigo tengo mi mejor amigo, mi cervesita, (*here in my hand is my best friend, my beer*)." He pulled out a crumpled piece of paper from his pocket and leaned in to show it to me. "Everyday I play the lotto so one day I can buy back my father's land."

His name was Miguel. When I told him I was Puerto Rican too, he proceeded to tell me that "Nuyoricans" and "Puerto Ricans" did not mean the same thing. He wasn't negative just schooling me on the difference between the two, saying that many of the cultural traditions are not honored in the states the same way they are in Puerto Rico. Miguel also expressed that he felt people back home were more humble and appreciative of their simple life. Whereas here in the city, he found that the youth would take things for granted, namely their parents. I started to take offense to some of the things he was saying, and then realized, it was only his opinion and it was true in his experience.

I finally understood where he was coming from when he shared a story with me about how some American settlers had offered him what he thought was a good price for acres of land he owned. He was a simple man with no knowledge of what it was worth, so when he was offered twenty-five grand for it, he believed it was a good deal because they told him it was. People from the island are trustworthy and naive. Whereas here in the states we can come off as guarded. Years later when he went to visit his hometown, it turned out that the twenty-grand he accepted was nothing compared to the multi-millions that it really was worth. I later learned that in the 1940s, lots of farmers were forced to sell their land to U.S. sugar companies for pennies on the dollar.

Miguel said he looked around and saw that the natural environment he once grew up in was now long gone. Replaced by hotels and apartment complexes. Something similar had happened to my own grandpa many years ago, and as a result, he died poor.

Miguel crinkled his head in a kind of daze as if remembering a time from his distant past. He pulled out an old photo of him from his wallet.

"I was born and raised in Vieques and I miss it." "Then go back, or shut up!" the boy dissed as he turned up the volume on his boom box.

"You shut up! You think that Spanglish is our language and rap is our music and it's not! Respect. You are young enough to be my grandchild." He flung his wrist in the boy's general direction as he toddled off at the next stop.

I was fuming inside. I already had an insight into what he had lived through. Who knows who he left behind? What else was taken from him? Someone had to take a stand, and today that person would be me.

At the next station, a couple of more teens hopped onto the train. The clan of them all gathered around this 15-year-old girl with a high-pitched screechy voice talking loudly as if she was doing some type of stand-up routine.

"Yo, so I think Scooby Doo was Dominican, 'cause he was dark-skinned. Plus 'cause of his accent, no one understood him when he talked. And I don't care what anybody says, Yogi Bear was smokin' weed-uhhuh, 'cause he always had the munchies and there was a white cop always chasin' him. And another thing, what the hell is up with the McDonald's crew of characters? They are so creepy; The Hamburgler, Ronald and what the fuck is Grimace? He's like a deformed Barney dinosaur. And what about superhero's like Aquaman? He was just stupid. What kind of a superhero can fight crime if he's always chillin' under water with the fish?" She sucked her teeth, then put on a pair of knock-off Chanel sunglasses.

"If I were a superhero, I would be Ghetto Fabulous Girl! I would save anybody out there who looked busted! You gotta look good or else nobody will take you serious. Everybody on this train is in need of a serious makeover." She flashed everyone her extremely long hot pink painted nails.

"I just got my nails done too, they're all mine except

for this...and this one," she ranted as she gave everyone the finger. Then she had begun to float around the subway car pointing out all the people who she felt were ugly as the music played. Finally, she started to sing along to the tune on her friend's boom box. Everyone seemed to ignore her and her little friend, but I had heard enough and was ready to unleash my inner bitch.

"Can you shut the fuck up? No one gives a shit about who you are or what you wanna be!"

To spite me, her little sidekick raised the volume even louder on the boom box. I yanked it away and smashed it on the floor. He looked as if he was going to cry. "Yo, lady! My brother gave this to me before he went to Iraq." He picked it up to try to put it together. For a second, I felt bad. As I took a good look at him, I noticed he must have only been about thirteen years old. I don't know what came over me. My assignment was to do one major bitchy thing a day, and aside from claiming my seat, this was it. "You better watch out, stupid lady, or I'll cut you with my nails..." I laughed at the girl's attempt to be bold.

"Go ahead, do it. I dare you." I slowly walked toward her not breaking eye contact, like a hungry lioness eyeing her prey. "Yo, you crazy." she shrugged.

"You know who else don't give a shit about you? You're parents. They obviously don't care about you because you use this subway as your place to shine... I may be crazy and that old man may be old, but you're gonna be a nobody, and that is forever." I insulted.

The other teens surrounding her and her little friend were quiet, one of 'em even started to giggle. I had successfully bullied the subway bully.

I felt good until I saw the young boy reach toward the girl and give her a hug. She had started to silently cry. The people on the train looked at me stunned. How could I be the shocking one on the train? What the hell just happened? Why is it that when you give people a taste of their own medicine, it's not as gratifying? I didn't mean to make that girl cry. I knew nothing about why these young kids were acting up like that to begin with. Maybe they didn't even have parents.

When I got off the subway, I walked home from the station feeling guilty knowing that I had gone too far. Although I had accomplished my goal of becoming the biggest bitch on the train that day, it didn't feel good.

While I laid in bed that night, I stared at the ceiling and wondered how anyone could be both bitchy and loving at the same time. Then the answer came to me. You can't. It's either one or the other. Being sweet and sour only works well when it's my favorite soup.

The shame of that day haunted me as I tried to figure out how to be a more balanced person like a good stand-up comedian who seems to address issues boldly and not directly attack anyone. Then I remembered my aunt telling me as a kid that in order to make a good tasting cup of coffee I had to add a little love. So I made that my focus for the upcoming days.

I was determined that it was going to be an exciting new day. Christmas time was near and I'd heard that an apartment became available in a building close to my school in Manhattan...and it was affordable. I had done enough odd jobs and saved enough money for me to be able to move on and finally venture out on my own. To be sure I was heading down the right path, I made an appointment to see a woman I was sure would steer me in the right direction. When you have an issue, you can pay big bucks to see a therapist or, you can pay $20 and do what most Nuyoricans do, go to a *Santera*.

"They call me Dona Luz because I show people the light. Not the light you see when you die, the light meaning the truth. Which to a lot of people is scarier than dying, because they come to me thinking I'm gonna tell them what they want to hear." she shared.

Dona Luz had her tiny spiritual shop in the Bronx. She wore a long white puffy dress, with her hair wrapped in a white turban. Everything about her outfit was blindingly white, blue-tinged by Tide, the detergent of choice for most Latinos.

She was tan and had very expressive dark brown eyes that seemed to bore a hole through my soul. Her Bronx accent was so thick that you could only understand it if you'd lived in New York for a while. As she prepared her table for me, she shared some of her stories to put me at ease.

"One woman wanted me to do a brujo (*cast a spell*) so her cheating man would only love her. I said, forget all that. Get even with the son of a bitch. I gave her this..." She pulled out a pink candle in the shape of a man, with a wick for a penis.

"I told her to light this candle and call me in the morning. And for his Dueña Sucia..." (*dirty mistress*).

She pulled out a matching candle of a voluptuous woman whose nipples had two white cotton string nubs that you could also light.

"Another time I had this loco from around here pay me $1000 cash, so I could make the Yankees win the World Series. Thank God they won, because I bought myself this really nice living room set." I glanced at my watch. She caught me.

"Anyway, get naked and stand over there." I was confused, I heard about people reading auras and stuff, but

I had to bare my privates? By the storefront window for all to see?

She could sense my concern. She started rattling on about the stupidity of some of her untrusting customers. I wasn't sure if she was on my side or if she was daring me to submit and become as gullible as the rest of them.

I stepped out of my clothes sheepishly. I was already humiliated, but I couldn't make myself run away. If I was going to be on my own once and for all, I had to do what she said so I forced myself to be open to the experience.

I was pulled in by the scent of incense as she placed two brass cups on the table. When she bumped into them with her shell bracelets, they chimed. She then poured wine in one cup and water in the other. In the background sounds of Afro-Cuban folk music played. I could feel the sounds of the drums penetrate my body. Suddenly I felt myself get very still. The sensation of a strong presence was near. Dona Luz looked me up and down and started shaking her head. She took a step back and crossed herself.

"You got a lot of negativity in your aura and I need to clean it off." she said inspecting me from head to toe.

I wondered if she was going to bust out with soap and water and wash me, but instead she called out to her assistant who was in the basement.

"Ramon, bring me two cantaloupes, a pumpkin, café con leche, some rice with beans... and a chicken."

I was horrified. Was she gonna sacrifice an innocent chicken over my head? I reached for my coat. She crossed her arms. "That's not for a sacrifice, those are my groceries."

She pulled out these long twigs with big leaves on the end of them from the top shelf. "These are called *lucky leaves* in Spanish they're called Ganchos. I'm gonna clean you with them. It's gonna hurt and you won't feel so lucky, but they'll work."

She walked around me in a clockwise direction as she whacked me several times with the leaves. "Pa fuera! Go! Cleanse!" she chanted. The last one really stung. As she bent down to clean up the leaves and twigs that had fallen to the floor after my beating, she sprinkled some holy water on my head.

"You know Jonisha, a lot of people look at me and think I'm all about killing chickens. But, that's not what my religion is about." She paused and looked me dead in the eye. "I kill other things—goats, pigeons—but let me tell you something, I'm just as close to God as any of those people standing on the street preaching about Jesus. It's about your intention and your faith."

She wrapped me in a towel and had me sit by a little table. Then Dona Luz spit Jack Daniels at my feet and blew cigar smoke in my face. People walked by the storefront window as if there was nothing odd about a half-naked girl with red welts sitting there.

"Okay now, shuffle the cards and cut them in three." The cards sitting on the table didn't look like fancy tarot cards I'd see during Halloween. No, these were more like a regular deck of playing cards. She stared at me and read my mind. "You want me to use the other cards, I have those too. It's the same thing, watch." At least with a more familiar deck of cards, I'd be able to make my own assessment. Dona Luz pulled out these obnoxiously huge Rider-Waite tarot cards from a box under the table. After I had shuffled them a few times, the first card she pulled was the ten of swords. It was one of the goriest cards in the deck showing a man lying dead in the snow with ten swords lodged in his back and blood all over.

"Do you sometimes feel like you're being chased and you don't know by what?" I nodded yes.

She pointed at the card. "Well, this card says that in your last life, you were a cucaracha and somebody squashed your ass. See? The swords in your back stand for how many people stepped on you. Let that go."

It all seemed to make sense. I made a mental note that I was no longer a roach in this life. Phew!

"Only kidding. The Spirits are telling me to tell you not to be afraid. Just relax. What this card is saying is that you're old self is dying. Which means you've been through some tough opportunities for growth. And there is more to come." I was confused, it was obvious that this card meant for me to watch my back at all costs, I didn't see any opportunities in that. She clarified. "The pictures on the cards aren't always meant to be literal.

As a reader, I go by vibe and what my spirit guides say. So that is what it means." She flipped over another card. "Do you feel lonely; touching yourself, pretending your hand is Mr. Right? Well, I got good news and bad news for you. The bad news is Mr. Right isn't coming anytime soon. The good news? You got two hands. Have fun." she said seriously.

She held up the three of swords, a heart with three swords pierced through it, behind it streaks of sunshine. I rolled my eyes. I guess that explained why I hadn't found a boyfriend yet.

When she flipped over the last card she paused and shook her head. She looked at it very seriously, before interpreting it. "This is why I prefer using my other deck of cards. Now don't be scared..." When she showed me the card, it was the infamous death card, a drawing of a skeleton behind a long black cloak with gleaming red eyes standing before a boat taking away innocents.

"I predict an ending is near. A big change for you is coming." I smiled and just knew she had to be talking about my new apartment.

"I see here, you already escaped death. You got lucky. I also see you on a stage with money. Cash... Are you some kind of an exotic dancer or a prostitute?"

I shook my head no. "I see an opportunity, and a blessing coming your way. Be on the lookout for it." I was happy to hear that since my employment situation was so inconsistent. "Blessings, endings or even death can always be our greatest teacher. Pay attention or you will miss it. I'm done." I smiled and I knew I was ready for what was to come.

*I*t was Christmas week and school was over for me until January. After filling out several applications for apartments, I had finally gotten approved for a small studio on the upper west side. It was time for me to break the news to my Titi Clara, who I had been avoiding. I had nothing remaining on my to-do list. For the first time in a long while, I sat with my aunt in the kitchen. I noticed she had large black and blue marks on her arms.

"Titi Clara, what happened?" I inquired.

"La vida me amor. You want some café?" she replied trying to change the subject.

As I studied my aunt, she seemed to be more tired than usual. I hadn't noticed that her hair was falling out. She was very pale and had lost some weight. I saw the counter top was lined with dozens of prescription medication bottles. Guiltily, I remembered the times doctors would leave voice messages for her and I would skip over them to retrieve mine instead.

"The cancer is back, mija. And this time it's not going away." She said with no emotion.

"Why didn't you tell me?" I asked.

"You have been very busy, running here and going there." she complained.

I didn't know what to say. How could I have been so unaware of what was going on? I suddenly felt bad, she needed me here and yet I was set to move within a week.

"I'm okay, I am not afraid. So don't you feel sorry for me." she reassured me sweetly as she handed me a cup of Joe. I smiled at her weakly. Inside I felt horrible. She sensed my sorrow, came over to me and put her hand on my shoulder. "Always remember that life is like a cup of café. Some days it may be too hot or taste too sweet, but most times, if you make it with love, it will be perfect." I sat there quietly savoring every sip of her famous coffee knowing that those cups of joy were numbered. "Good girl. The only way to enjoy it is to sit tranquilla (peacefully), and drink it. Then you will feel Gods love. I promise you."

We sat quietly in the kitchen. She got up to prepare some more coffee and then turned to me and said, "It's your turn." We smiled at each other then I jumped up ran to my room, opened my night drawer and pulled out the colador she had given me as a gift. I realized I had a bigger opportunity than just gaining my independence by moving out, or getting a job. I had a chance to serve a woman who was a wife, a mother, a loving friend and a true believer in God.

That day I made her my very first, and very best cup of café con leche.

"Delisioso." she complimented as it went down smoothly. We both appreciated its creamy warmth. Although I didn't tell her with words, I wanted her to know that I loved her immensely and hoped she felt it emanating from me.

With all that caffeine in our systems, we ended up sitting in that kitchen for hours talking about everything. I even told her my story about losing my dog JR as a kid, and being robbed. I told her about the seminar and the subway. And then I disclosed to her my plans about the apartment and how I was scheduled to move in very soon. Titi was genuinely happy for me. Only I wasn't so thrilled about it anymore. I realized I had spent so much of my time focused on getting away that I hadn't even acknowledged that my aunt's place had become my home too.

Before I went to bed, I gave her a big hug. Magically, although it didn't reverse her cancer, my faith had been renewed. I felt the presence of love surrounding me. Maybe it was the coffee. I said a prayer for my aunt's recovery. Then I pulled the small photo of Jesus out of the drawer and tucked it under my pillow. As I was dozing off, she came into my room and gave me a kiss on my forehead. "Good Night mi amor. Oh And have a Merry Christmas and Happy New Year."

"Um…Christmas isn't until next week but Feliz Navidad to you too Titi." I teased as I shut off the light.

And that was the last time I saw my Titi Clara. Early the next morning, I awoke to a loud thump coming from the kitchen. When I heard it, intuitively I knew what it was. A lump swelled in my throat as tears welled in my eyes. I jumped out of bed and there lying on the kitchen floor was Titi Clara's peaceful lifeless body, in her hand- the colador.

I sat in the apartment alone, packing up some of my aunt's belongings. I looked around at all of the elephant figurines that were finally free to live elsewhere.

When I gained my independence, it wasn't how I expected. Turns out, Titi Clara owned her apartment, and in the end, she left it to me.

Tucked inside my night drawer was an envelope I'd never seen before. When I opened it, I saw that inside was a collection of my small monthly rental contributions along with a little note that said "Apaga la luz. Te Quiero." Tears streamed down my cheeks and I smiled to myself hearing her nightly phrase echoed in my ear for the last time.

I finally had my own place; only this time I was missing the one person that made it home. Although I was grateful and humbled, I felt alone. I promised myself I would start fresh. I wouldn't try to force life to be what I wanted it to be.

At the funeral service the following week, I couldn't stop crying. Afterwards I went for a walk hoping to find inner peace. Just then, I saw a man walking a little black and white dog. A Shitzu, like the one I had when I was a kid. He managed to get away from his owner and ran directly towards me. I kneeled down and pet him remembering how my dad once said that "dog" spelled backwards is "God." A big smile formed on my face because in that moment I realized that I wasn't alone after all. I felt God was indeed with me, and so was my Titi Clara.

Epilogue

I got a call from someone who wanted to hire me to be a clown to read stories at the Children's Hospital. Since the last party I worked turned out to be a disaster, I was ready to turn this gig down. Then something inside told me to take it; after all it was at a children's hospital.

When I arrived at the hospital, the nurse told me to wait while she gathered the kids. I fixed my wig, adjusted my clown nose and when they brought the kids out, there in the middle was a familiar face. "Danny?" Turned out Danny had gotten leukemia. That day I put on my best performance for those kids. I even made peace with Danny's Mom, Paula, and made a promise to visit him every Saturday until his transition. I may have missed that opportunity with my aunt, but I wasn't about to with Danny.

When I got home, I made myself a fresh pot of coffee and sat at the kitchen table. I felt tremendous gratitude for all the things I now loved. I realized why my aunt was so passionate about her coffee. It gave her time to reflect and connect with that source of love within. There is so much to love in this world, so I pulled out a little journal and started to write down all the things I loved:

I love children, because they're honest, loving and true to themselves.

I love my family, because they helped shape who I have become.

I've learned to embrace death, because it reminds me to appreciate the people and pets that are here today, and may be gone tomorrow.

I love laughter, because when we laugh, who we really are shines through, if only for a moment. The truth is you can't hide who you are. We were all born naked and we're going naked and we can't take that self-created mask with us.

I put my pen down, closed my journal and looked out the window. I began to realize that I also loved all the people that I have met so far on this journey because they made me recognize one thing; that I do believe in God. When I remember I am not alone, I feel the love that is always present and I know *He's* here with me.

And last but not least, although we haven't met yet, I love you too, because you are now on the inside of what I once showed no one...ME

Nude in New York, NYC theatres

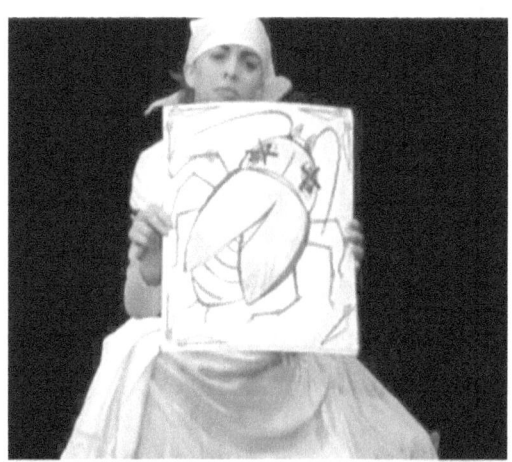

Bonus One-Act Play

The following is a one-act monologue show I produced at the Flight Theater in Los Angeles originally titled "It's not OK." With each transformation of the production, a new title is born thus this play has also been called "Empow-HER," "Insecurities," and most recently "Exposed." For this first production there were only three actors in my cast interchanging roles, Kelly Kinsella, Kristen Moser, and me. I was thrilled to be able to work with these amazingly talented women.

This piece was created as a result of a writing workshop I taught where a group of women explored the dynamics of insecurities at their jobs and in their relationships. My original intent with this play was to have a theatrical piece I could direct with a diverse cast of women.

This particular version of my play represents where it was at that specific time and is always evolving as I continue to fine tune stories and add more to it. I thought it would be fun to include it in this book because the theme and subject matter fit together nicely. It also gave me an opportunity to complete my healing theatrical collection of works called, "The Naked Series."

It has been my pleasure sharing my words with you. Enjoy.

EXPOSED

OVERLOOKED AND UNDERESTIMATED

Music cue: Don't' Let Me Get Me, by Pink.

(Lights up. A group of women gather together on stage in front of the curtain. Each carries a silk red scarf. They put them on slowly in a way that's unique to them. MICHELLE, THE MOM, steps forward away from the ladies and gazes into the audience. She wears her red scarf wrapped around her shoulders. The ladies slowly disappear behind her off-stage. Once the gals are gone, the music fades and Michelle speaks to the audience.)

MICHELLE

I think it's safe to say that most of us have at one point or another felt overlooked underestimated and sometimes even ignored. For me, it happened during recess when I was in the third grade. When team captains were chosen for a game of kickball, I was the last to be picked. I had always been a good kicker and couldn't understand what it was about me that made them choose me last.

As I timidly took my place on the team, the kids started to groan. When it was finally my turn to kick, to my surprise I kicked that ball so far out of the field that our team earned an extra two points and we won the game. Needless to say, the groans transformed into cheers and the team win had resulted in me being chosen first the next time around.

Turns out that wasn't gonna be the only time this type of scenario would pop up in my life. As I grew up there were countless other moments where insecurity and fear reared its ugly head. Usually it was provoked from the outside in. I'd either observe something that bugged me, or someone would say something that felt off thus creating self-doubt within me. Or worse I would be blatantly rejected. At times the uncertainties and fears were small and would go away quickly. And other times they'd be overwhelming causing anxiety.

So I set out to meet women, who like me, had stories to share about how they dealt with their insecurities. I decided to record their tales because I've always believed that as we listen to others a piece of us can be healed. Which is my hope for you as you follow me on this journey.

The first woman to open up to me was Victoria. *(The names have been changed to protect the guilty.)* She was a career woman in her late fifties who was being forced to retire from her place of employment after putting in twenty years.

Victoria had been a dedicated employee and couldn't understand for the life of her why this was happening now. That is, until the day she met her replacement. It was then that she chalked up the sudden change to the fact that she was no longer "eye candy."

(MICHELLE exits the stage.)

REPLACED

(Curtain opens to reveal VICTORIA, THE EMPLOYEE, seated on a chair smoking a cigarette on a bare stage. She has her red scarf tied around her chest.)

VICTORIA

She was the youngest woman sitting in the waiting room and right away I knew she was my replacement. My boss walked by us and she shot him a flirtatious look followed by a smirk. He blushed which made him trip and bump into me. I've known his wife, Lorraine, for many years so I took offense at the exchange they assumed was just between them. I scanned her from head to toe and then introduced myself.

"Hi, I'm Victoria. You must be Britney. *[Beat]* Congratulations on getting hired here, good job! I see that out of thirty five middle-aged applicants, you are officially the one taking over my position." I couldn't help but notice her incredibly large breasts. After glaring at them I said, "Wow, your boobs are huge! I admire that. What are they size double D? They are so perky. How long did it take for them to stretch your perfect porcelain skin to fit those beach balls? *(She takes a long drag on her cigarette, then casually blows smoke in the air.)* I can already tell that you are going to fit in here just fine. Follow me." I snickered.

"Anyway Boobies, I'd like to finish up this tour as quickly as possible so I can get to happy hour. So here are the basics, you start at 6 a.m. sharp and your hours will be late... very late. They say you will have your weekends free, but that is a lie. Your life is now your job. Be sure to bring an overnight bag. This cabinet here on your right holds colored paper for faxes and the one on the left has basic supplies."

As I escorted Boobies around the office, I stopped and observed a wall that had been nicely decorated with framed photos of my co-workers and me at various office parties throughout the year. That was when I broke down in tears. Like a warm wool sweater that no longer fits, it had occurred to me that I no longer fit at my job. My co-workers like that sweater, kept me warm because over time they became like my family. And soon they'd become strangers.

I turned to Brittany and for a moment I felt like I was looking in the mirror at a younger version of me. I said, "Boobies, one day you'll wake up and wonder where the time went. You'll realize your life has passed you by and you didn't fulfill a single one of your dreams because you got comfortable with where you were.

"I can tell by looking at you that you don't think you will ever age. Chances are most of what you've gotten in life was handed to you because of your looks. But guess what? They don't last. One day you'll wake up with crows feet around your eyes, and laugh lines on your face, and the only things on your body that you will recognize are those implants you paid for. *(She takes another drag of her cigarette).* Or maybe that's just my story."

I didn't mean to be such a bitch but I was hurt, Michelle. I felt like I no longer had anything to live for. To make matters worse it wasn't like I had belonged to any work union that could save my job like so many others my age. On my way to the office that morning I woke up to the fact that it was time for me to move on and I didn't want to let go.

Originally my goal was to work there for 3 to 5 years max and then get out into the world with a nice savings stashed. Thing is, I got comfortable. Now here it is some 20 years later and I didn't do a damn thing. That's when I realized maybe the universe was forcing me to move on so I could finish what I set out to do in the first place. What if this is just a sign that better options are coming my way if just "Let Go and

Let God?"

I may be a fifty-six-year-old single woman with no kids and a shelved NYU degree, but I'm not dead yet. *(She rises from her chair and removes her scarf.)*

I think it's time I make good use of that degree. Who knows maybe someday Boobies... *(She clears her throat.)* I mean Brittany will come and work for me.
(VICTORIA drops her cigarette to the floor nd crushes it with the heel her shoe before she exits off-stage. MICHELLE re-enters.)

MICHELLE

Victoria paid for our brunch and saw me to my car. Nine months later she had opened up her own temp agency. Brittany became her assistant. *(MICHELLE exits proudly.)*

THE FLAKE

Music cue: I'm Coming Out, by Diana Ross

(THE FLAKE enters swiftly carrying her own stool. She puts it down and sits on it. Her red scarf is wrapped around her neck.)

CANDACE

To some people, I'm known as "The flake." It's a label I was unfairly given when I allowed myself to be bullied into saying yes to a commitment, after I had initially said no. You see for me it's not what you say, it's how you feel when you say what you say. You follow me? If someone says, "yes," from a place of feeling like "no," then the answer is still gonna be "no," regardless of what that someone was forced to agree to.

Look, I'm not suggesting that people go around breaking their word. That's obviously rude and disrespectful to your friends, family and to yourself. All I'm saying is that I prefer to remain in integrity with the decisions I set out for myself from the get-go and I shouldn't be shamed for it. Make sense?

Anyway, Clarinda and I met at a business-networking event. Although I'd seen her at the job in passing, she worked in a different department than I did so we didn't know each other. In time she introduced me to some of her other friends and we became buddies. We'd go out for drinks occasionally and workout at the gym. Problem was, I never felt good about myself around Clarinda and her clique of friends. It always seemed like her perception of me dominated how the others treated me. These women loved to point out my imperfections as if they were trying to help me fix my problem. "No shit I have a zit on my face, asshole! I see it every day." I'd say to myself all pissed-off.

When I was finally invited to Clarinda's house party I didn't want to go. But because I felt pressured to, I did. I arrived and stayed for a bit, then left early so I could get home in time to feed my cats. Thing is, I forgot my purse. So I go back and I'm about to knock on the door when something interesting happened. I began to hear these women cackling like witches on the other side of that door. The more they laughed, the more curious I became. That's when I heard a familiar name and discovered what they were laughing at... ME! They were baggin' on me—saying the most messed up crap.

They talked about how I looked. And because I'm Asian, they remarked on my features and said stupid racist shit like "Why didn't she bring the egg rolls?" I mean it was fucked up. They even complained about how they couldn't believe I brought cheap wine.

When they finally let themselves out of the house, they froze when they saw me standing there, like school kids that had just been caught writing on the wall with sharpies.

That's when I knew I had to confront them and cut them off once and for all. I took a deep breath and then this power came over me as I let each of them have it. *(She loosens up her scarf.)*

"How dare you! All of you! You think I wanted to be here tonight. No! I was perfectly fine with watching reruns of *Friends,* alone."

"Clarinda, I was there for you when you were going through your painful divorce. I even called out of work sick so I could stay with you and cheer you up. Yet, whenever I needed you to lean on, you were nowhere to be found. You know why, because you're an asshole and you only care about yourself." I pushed her to the side and faced Judy next.

"Judy, no one will say it to your face, but you're an alcoholic. Get help. You have some nerve making fun of me for bringing cheap wine when that didn't stop you from drinking it! Stop believing you are an occasional drinker because morning, noon and night, is all fucking day sweetie." Judy shamefully looked away as I turned to Samantha.

"Samantha, I'm obviously just your token minority pal. Admit it, you like be around me so you can prove to the world that you are associated with an Asian. You're a closet racist!

"You're all mean spirited people. Like a female version of 'The Grinch.' Your perceptions of me are not my reality. If you refuse to see my greatness, even in my moments of weakness, you are no friend of mine. If you like to assume that I am not educated because that makes you feel smarter, then you are no friend of mine. If you get a kick out of putting me or anyone else down for the thrill of it, you are no friend of mine.

I barged out of Clarinda's place with my empty bottle of wine in one hand, and my dignity in the other. That night I forgave myself for believing I was unworthy and for surrounding myself with people that would continue to validate that opinion. What they think of me is no longer any of my business. And for the record, I have never been late or flaked out on a commitment since.

(CANDACE exits stage left to the sound of Diana Ross. She takes the stool with her.)

MR. POTENTIAL

(SOPHIA MARKS, THE WIFE, enters from the stage right wing. She's wearing a red scarf as a blind-fold. She removes it. A shocked look forms on her face.)

SOPHIA

"Arnold, you Idiot!" *(She screams looking out into the audience as if she's yelling directly at him. Sophia then paces back and forth. She faces another direction to speak to Michelle.)*

I was driving around town running errands all day while my husband insisted on staying home to surf the Internet to look for a job. I was at a stoplight about to turn onto the freeway when something told me to go back home. Then all of a sudden, I had a full on anxiety attack. I have come to learn that you need to pay attention when your heart is trying to tell you something. So, I hauled ass home and walked into the living room and found the one thing I was afraid to face, him fucking another woman.

I looked over at this redheaded girl covering herself with a blanket and immediately recognized her as our waitress from the Olive Garden.

The one my husband complimented for her "great service." Unbeknownst to me he had also gotten her cell phone number. Can you believe it? I calmly turned to her and asked, *(She looks toward mistress,)* "Oh my, is that an earring in your you-know-what? *(She turns back to Arnold.)* Wow, she's a real winner Arnold."

You know what Michelle, I had been such a fool. A friend once told me that if I had an issue with someone the best way to handle it was to weigh the pros and cons by writing them down. After filling up two notebooks with cons about our marriage, you think I would have left his ass back then. I wondered why I stayed so long and could never find the answer until it hit me like a ton of bricks right then and there. I said to him,

"I figured it out! I fell in love with your 'potential' Arnold, and all the things I thought you could become. You are not good for me. 'Mr. Potential' would never cheat. He's courageous enough to tell me if he isn't interested in what he's got. Plus, he's too busy being amazing."

Michelle, I kept going over it in my head and beating myself up over his fascination with other women to the point where I actually started to believe I wasn't pretty or good enough. I even assumed my cooking was bad? And that is not true! *(SOPHIA stands on her chair.)* I'M A FABULOUS COOK! MY EGGPLANT PARMIGIANA IS BETTER HIS MOTHERS!" *(She clears her throat and takes a deep breath and steps down. She is visibly calmer.)*

I walked over to him and said,

"I think it's time we stop pretending everything is great between us. Go be with a woman that is okay with you just as you are, because I'm not. I do expect you to be the best you can be. I do expect you to aim higher. I do expect you to want to sleep with me more than once in a blue moon. And I do expect you to honor the vows that you made to me under God.

You know what screw 'Mr. Potential'. Maybe by leaving you, 'Mr. Certain' will finally be able to find me, 'Mrs. Amazing and Available.' *(She turns her head the direction of the mistress.)*

"Waitress, keep him. If you are pathetic enough to pursue a man who will never fully commit to you, then go for it. Just don't be shocked when you wind up all alone wishing someone would love you only to discover they only love the pleasures you provide. Karma is a bitch. *(Sophia turns back to address the husband.)*

"Arnold, I can put up with sneaky but now your sneakiness looks more like a coward's behavior to me. And my 'Mr. Certain', is not a coward. He's a man who fights for what he believes in, like his marriage. He not only cherishes his wife, he's also committed to her because he's *certain* she's the one for him."

Before he left, I strongly considered attacking the redhead with my flat iron and claiming my man. But then I came to my senses. Look, if you are with someone who isn't happy being with you, why keep holding on? Let go already so you can attract someone who is better for you, right?

On his way out, he turned to me with tears in his eyes and gave me a kiss on the cheek. It was finally done and even though ours was a slightly dramatic ending, I'm okay that it's over. I believe in my heart there is someone out there who will appreciate and adore me and I refuse to settle anymore.

(Lights out. SOPHIA leaves.)

THE FALL

Music cue: Autumn in New York, by Billie Holiday

(Stagehands bring out a small bed and set it downstage right. MICHELLE walks in carrying a laptop and stands next to the bed.)

MICHELLE

Sophia Marks had embraced a new season of change in her life. She was now truly ready for real love to come to her because she loved herself enough to let go of the relationship that was holding her back. *(MICHELLE makes herself comfortable on the bed. Before she opens her laptop she studies the leaf printed quilt. Music fades out.)*

MICHELLE

This is the time of year when you can see the leaves falling off the trees as you gaze out the window. A time when cozy quilts are taken out of the closet along with long boots you can't wait to wear again. There is something so special about the fall. I love how the cool wind lightly kisses you upon the cheek. The colors of the leaves are inspiring. As I take in each uniquely shaped leaf, like snowflakes in the winter, I appreciate their beauty and perfection.

During the fall the birds seem happier, the squirrels are friendlier. And it's cool enough outside for a light jacket, but not so cold that you are forced to stay inside. And yet, some nights staying inside is just what's needed to refresh myself. Particularly on days I'm not feeling so hot. I go from feeling great about myself one moment, to feeling not so awesome within the next. Even on a good make-up day, I will look into every mirror I pass by just to be sure my make-up didn't wear off to reveal Godzilla.

Then I remember how perfect the leaves are on the trees. How the flowers exude their own special beauty. And I realize, I'm no different than any of God's other precious living things.

Yet on those days that I feel and look good, no man or woman should feel entitled to touch me. And if they do, I have a right to do something about it, especially if it feels off to me. I know of many beautiful women who rarely stick up for themselves when a compliment or seemingly innocent touch, becomes harassment. Like a rose, once it's plucked, it slowly begins to die. The flowers out in the garden are more beautiful when they are admired from a distance and left alone.

I have been faced with sexual harassment ever since I was a kid, but the day a scraggly old teacher hit on me things changed.

I had gone to school to drop off a paper that I had forgotten to turn in and as I was reaching into my bag, this fool had shut the door trapping us alone in the empty classroom. I felt awkward as he rubbed his body into mine and pushed himself into my breasts. As I agitatedly looked for a way to escape he grabbed me by the waist.

It was horrible. He was old enough to be my grandfather. His teeth were yellow and his breath smelled like dirty diapers! Mr. Warden was also very strong. So many thoughts raced through my mind like how if I screamed he could beat or rape me.

I started sweating, which apparently turned him on. He let out a groan. Ugh! It was so disgusting. I felt helpless.

I glanced over at a trophy sitting on the desk. I imagined grabbing it and hitting him repeatedly on the head with it knocking him to the floor so that I could escape. The whole time I prayed someone would walk in and save me.

And yet, I couldn't get the words out to save myself.

I was about to give up and surrender to him when luckily I heard the sound of a key unlocking the door. He quickly moved away from me and grabbed a folder as if reviewing some of the paperwork inside of it. I was relieved to see another woman, a teacher, had let herself in. She stared at us suspiciously for a moment. I smiled at her hoping she sensed my relief as I grabbed my bag and scurried out the door. Phew!

The next day although I debated skipping class, I went anyway. I wasn't about to let my schoolwork suffer. Afterwards he pulled me to the side and apologized profusely. Later that week I switched classes and Mr Warden never bugged me again.

In his mind, I supposedly sent out some kind of signal that led him to think that what he did was acceptable. I felt dirty and confused. Was is the Target jumpsuit I was wearing to class that day that got him off? Or was it my genuine smile I flashed to everyone that gave him the wrong impression?

I became determined to find the balance between owning and expressing my feminine energy like the flowers in the garden, while at the same time setting up boundaries that would be honored and respected by others; Like a lioness, I longed for that strength.

That's when I stumbled across Lacey online. She was a friend of a friend on Facebook that had her own group fan page called "For the Love of Me." On it were photos of her fabulous, plus-sized self, pole dancing.

When I witnessed Lacy's skills, I reached out to her right away. She was insanely talented. She also exuded the kind of confidence that made people think twice about approaching her disrespectfully.

Yes it's ironic that I'd befriend a pole dancer to help me keep the sharks away, but I could tell by Lacy's photos that she had a story to share that I could learn from. We began an online chat.

(The stage lights dim on MICHELLE as she continues to type on her laptop.)

INNER BEAUTY

Music cue: Miss Independent, by Ne-yo

(A sheer pink curtain opens upstage revealing an illuminated stripper pole. LACY, THE DANCER, a hot plus-sized woman spins seductively around the pole. Tied around her waist is her red scarf. Her moves are incredible as she incorporates the scarf into her routine. When the music ends, she puts on a robe. The rest of the monologue is played as if MICHELLE is chatting with LACY online.)

MICHELLE

It all started when I discovered, "pole dancing." It was marketed as a sexy exercise that was guaranteed to loosen you up in the bedroom and flatten your abs. So for shits and giggles I decided to take a class.

When I arrived for my first lesson, I was the fattest woman in the room. But I wasn't discouraged. The lights were dim enough that everyone in that studio looked good. The teacher demonstrated her moves and I was blown away. She floated around t hat p ole i n c ircles effortlessly with one arm! I on the other hand was afraid I'd strike oil twirling around that thing.

When it was my turn, I was a mess. I must

have fallen a dozen times. My knee popped out of place, I threw my back out, and my legs were covered in black and blues for weeks after. And you know what? I LOVED IT! I couldn't wait to go back for more. I had a blast! They even had sassy little costumes for everyone, including me. I could be a kitten, or even dress like a playmate with thigh high boots!

You'd be surprised how supportive the women are to each other in that type of environment. Some of them were strippers, others housewives. We learned so much but the main thing was how we handled ourselves when dancing. Like strippers at the club, they don't allow anyone to touch them without "value" being created for them first. You see, it's all about grace, control over your body, and eye contact. Those gals could be totally in the buff and eyes would be the only things that would fondle them.

I was so jazzed at how exhilarated I felt, bruises and all, that I set a goal to master the craft. The following week I purchased my very own at home stripper pole and began to document my exotic dancing experience on YouTube.

It didn't happen overnight though. In fact it took me almost two years to get really good. At first my husband Ernie rejected the whole thing.

Lucky for me he's never been the jealous type. We've been together since high school and are first and foremost very good friends.

When one of my web shows got two million hits and I started collecting checks, my dear old Ernie began to love what I do. Did you know that after a certain amount of views, YouTube actually pays you to put up videos? Well, my hubby and I were thrilled. Didn't lose much weight but my core is strong as hell. Believe me though, I wasn't always this confident.

When I was a kid, I remember asking my mom if she thought I was pretty. After a long silence she said, "Well you aren't the prettiest flower in the bouquet, but you are still my little flower just the same." At first the comment stung me like a bee. But then I chose to focus on how she at least saw me as a flower. And you know what? Ultimately, it didn't matter what she thought about me anyway.

On my webcam show I'm sultry and sensual and all the things no one believed I could be. *(She looks up to the heavens.)* Look out mom; I've bloomed into a beautiful rose bush.

Because I mastered a seemingly impossible task, I've inspired other women to be comfortable in their own skin. Best part is I'm making money, honey. I guess that makes me an "Entrepre-whore." Only kidding, they pay me well to promote classes.

Look honey bottom line is, predators out there are looking for victims not vixens. They want a woman they think they can prey on. Don't let that be you. Work on getting self-assured and before you know it, those types of people can't get near you, know what I mean? In fact, why don't you get yourself a full-length mirror and a pole so you can learn how to dance, honey? I promise you that your insecurity will disappear as you feel the rhythm of the music take control. It's like this power unleashes from within and before you know it, you begin to intimidate those with bad intentions.

My self-appreciation has grown and even improved my relationship with my hubby dramatically. Every day, hundreds of women give up on their lives simply because they've forgotten their beauty. "Life" is a precious gift. I'm bringing sexy back to the concept that breathing is enough. Aren't you happy to breathe? Aren't you grateful to be alive? Aren't you thankful that you are able walk, laugh, and use your eyes to see? Well, I am. And I'm even happier to dance.

(Lacy unties the scarf from around her waist and goes over to the pole. Sexy music plays again as she demonstrates one final trick. She suspends herself upside down in the air and looks dead into the audience.)

LACY

Go ahead unleash your hidden vixen!

MICHELLE

The next day I signed up for classes.

(Upstage sheer curtain closes; Michelle shuts her laptop and pulls the blankets over her head. Lights out.)

IT'S MY TURN

Music cue: Let's get Loud, by Jennifer Lopez

(In the darkness, MICHELLE hops out of bed. Stagehands enter set down a loveseat and leave taking the bed with them. When lights go up SHARON, THE LAWYER, stumbles in carrying two martini glasses. She plops down next to MICHELLE handing her a glass. Sharon's hair is in a bun and the red scarf is wrapped around it. Together they sip on their martinis and laugh. SHARON freezes in place. MICHELLE converses with the audience.)

MICHELLE

Sharon had guzzled down an apple martini before she shared her big secret with me. She was a lawyer that I became friends with after striking up a conversation during a kick-box class at the gym.

Sharon was the type of person that avoided making mistakes. Although she was enjoyable at times, she was usually more of the serious type. In most of her relationships, she was used to being in charge. And on this day, she seemed different, loose, and silly. It was nice to see her being so playful. What she shared next was scandalous for her. *(Sharon unfreezes and giggles like a schoolgirl before she shares her story.)*

SHARON

I met my lover for the first time at a tattoo shop after my appointment with the owner on a legal matter. On my way out my client, the owner, introduced me to his son who was just a couple of years younger than me. Well, his son was hot! He had these big green eyes and the best chiseled tattooed chest I have ever seen. It was the first time I ever wanted to bring a stranger home with me.

We exchanged numbers. At first our texting started off as casual flirting. Then it became full on *sexting*. I gave into my sexual desire, and we did it! Crazy right? His you know what, wasn't too big or too small, it was the perfect size. We fit together like a glove. There was no work involved in making me reach my orgasm. The pure animal gratification I felt was enough to get me off.

After he rocked me all night long I woke up surprised that I was capable of having an uninhibited one-night stand. I'm the good girl, the one that never broke a single rule in my household growing up. The one that didn't lose her virginity until she was twenty-three. The one who had only three boyfriends her whole life. *(She whispers the next line.)*

You wanna know why I'm so uptight? Unexpressed orgasms. Haven't had enough of em'. Who knew?

I never felt comfortable letting anyone in. After seeing what being open and loving did to my mom, I just couldn't bear getting into a relationship I couldn't control. Even though she died of cancer when I was a teen, I always believed it was her broken heart that did her in. She aimed to please my father and he just never noticed her efforts. It's one of the reasons I became an attorney to begin with. I wanted to be the voice for people like my mom who really didn't know how to articulate or even fight for what she wanted. I love my dad, but he was not a good fit for my sweet mother. She suffered as a result of it.

I turned to my "lover" and replied, "Oh my God, did we just do that?" I couldn't believe that I just jumped on top of this guy, and had my way with him. It felt great! I just cuddled with him and begged, "Please don't tell your father."

I wanted to enjoy my newfound sexual energy. It's not a crime right? I mean Michelle, I didn't feel a shred of guilt. In fact, suddenly I forgave myself for giving into my passion.

I also forgave my ex-boyfriend Luis, for all the stupid things he'd ever done, like cheating.

Hear me out, usually when a man cheats on a woman, she gets bent out of shape over it. It's the word "cheat" I have a problem with. As if being in a relationship was a made up game that consisted of winners, losers and cheaters. I mean the first thing I said when I found out I'd been deceived wasn't, "Oh my God I feel so betrayed" No, it was, "That asshole cheated on me." In other words "He got to play the game by his rules, not mine."

Read my lips. *(She points to her lips.)* Relationships are a game. If you want a monogamous partner, choose a monogamous player. If not you're setting yourself up to lose repeatedly. Look, I knew what I was getting myself into dating a charmer. It was my choice to play the game with Luis and since it didn't work out the way I wanted, I broke it off with him.

Who knows, maybe some men cheat because they are only doing what makes them happy in the moment. When he's ready to choose me as his one and only, he'll propose. Until then, I won't hide behind my work anymore. I'm gonna live a little too.

As I was looking at this gorgeous man lying

in my bed, I realized I was happy in that moment. So happy I forgot his name so I just called him Lover. I snuggled into him and said with a purr, "Lover, I want to thank you. Before last night, adventure came to me in the form of my chosen career."

Last night, I got to experience complete surrender to a man for the first time. It was great to feel what it was like allowing a man to express his masculine energy. When *Lover* touched my body something came over me and I just let go!

These days I wear my hair loose, put on sexy panties and perfume just because. Funny thing is, I never did that for myself before. I don't know why I never just tried being this way with Luis. Since when did I become his mom?

There was something about having this one-night-stand that made me appreciate life's little surprises. It was so exciting for me that I decided it's time to honor the feminine woman I was born to be.

(SHARON unties the red scarf from her head releasing the bun and shakes her hair loose. MICHELLE stands and speaks to the audience.)

MICHELLE

Sharon had finally tapped into her feminine energy and continued to see her "Lover" secretly until the passion between them fizzled out. About a few months later Luis came back into her life and proposed. This time they were ready for a real commitment. I attended the wedding and she is now pregnant with her first child. A little girl.

(Lights out. MICHELLE and SHARON skip off-stage.)

FAMILY GAL

Music cue: Come To My Window, By Melissa Etheridge

(House lights go up. A Butch looking lesbian woman named TATIANNA, THE NEWLYWED, is seated in the audience wearing a white tuxedo. Her red scarf is tied around her head like a bandana. When the music begins to fade, she rises from her seat and points at an audience member with a smile.)

TATIANNA

Suzy, you have been by my side through it all, and I love you more today than ever before. I'm so happy you are officially my wife. Those people protesting outside don't respect God because they don't acknowledge that true love is about the soul of person, not the male or female body it's housed in. *(She addresses another audience member as if he was Father Rivera.)*

Father Rivera you truly are a man of our Lord. I'm so grateful to you for marrying Suzy and I. It takes a lot of balls to go against the norm. I thought for sure you'd run, but instead you put your judgment aside because you cared enough about me as a person to make sure this day was special. Most importantly, you honored my choice. You will soar with the angels my friend.

I'm not really good with the speeches, so I'll make it quick. I love and appreciate all of you, period. No one may believe me but I came into this world as a man trapped in a woman's body. And although I could've accepted the female body I was gifted, it just didn't work out that way for me.

It ain't easy being gay in a world that wants to make you wrong for falling in love with someone of the same sex. For years I kept to myself for fear of being ridiculed and then I met my soul mate. From then on I didn't care because she actually brought me closer to God by teaching me that love is love and it doesn't matter what package it comes in. *(She turns and talks to another audience member.)*

Pop, you used to buy me toy cars for my birthday, *(She turns to someone else,)* and mom remember prom? Even though you wanted me in one of your handmade dresses, you got me a suit instead because that's what I wanted.

The rules about marriage back in the day were more about procreation. People got married to have kids, period. If they were in love, then it was a bonus. *[Beat]* I'm proud to announce that I'm pregnant. *[Beat.]* Ha! Gotcha! Actually we adopted a dog named Pete. Now we are one big happy family.

Most people can't wait to grow up and move far away from their families. Not me. When I wanted to play with toy cars instead of dolls, you let me, when I chose pantsuits over dresses nobody said one bad word about it. And when I came here to City Hall today to get married during a protest against my marriage, you showed up and pushed those protesters aside. Man oh Man that act alone fills my heart with joy. I love you all. This is for you!

(TATIANNA raises her glass to toast the audience. She takes a sip then passes ELIZABETH, THE BRIDE, as she dances off the stage.)

IT'S MY DAMN DAY!

Music cue: The Wedding March plays softly in the background.

(At the start of the song, ELIZABETH, THE BRIDE, marches along on stage wearing a wedding gown with her red scarf used as a veil. During the song, she yanks her veil off angrily.)

ELIZABETH

Okay, stop the music! *(Music abruptly cuts off.)* This wedding is a complete disaster. *(She addresses the audience as a group.)* This isn't working. This is the worst wedding I have ever attended. I recently went to a "homo" friend's wedding and hers was way better than this. *(Leans toward the audience singling out a woman in the center.)*

Mom, are you painting your nails right now? Are you serious? *(She hops off stage and charges at an audience member seated in the front row.)* Give me that nail polish right now! *(Elizabeth mimes grabbing a small bottle away from the person, then tosses it across the theatre.)* I can't believe you! It's bad enough you sucked as a parent. You think for one day you could stop being so self- absorbed? *(She spots another person from the corner of her eye, doing something else that bugs her.)*

Dad? Oh my God! Are those headphones in your ears? *(She rages over to someone and rips off imaginary headphones from their head, then stomps on them.)*

You and your damn sports! Can't you go one day without watching a football game? *(She paces back and forth.)* For once can the two of you at least go the extra mile for your only child?

You're the reason I wanted to get rescued by my "Knight in Shining Armor" in the first place and move out.

The one good thing you did in front of me was to show each other affection. As a result I prayed for my prince to come. And guess what? After patiently waiting all these years, I've had no such luck finding Mr. Right.

Women have all been taught by society not to settle when it comes to men. You're expected to keep waiting until the perfect person comes along. Never mind the fact that we ladies all have biological clocks ticking. So that's why I made this wedding happen. I'm not waiting anymore.

I met Herby here at the local car wash and you know what? He was the only one down to be my husband. Don't laugh! It's entirely possible this can become something that lasts forever. Right sweetheart? *(She turns to the imaginary Groom right next to her.)*

Honey, light of my life, what good is showing up as my groom to say, "I do", if you are making eyes at my fucking bridesmaid the whole time? *(She throws her bouquet to the floor and throws her hands in the air.)*

Truth is people we are broke. Herby agreed to marry me for the gifts. And just look at this table! What do you see? NOTHING! Not even a handmade greeting card. Really? Is that what you think of us? I could've really used that foot massager.

Am I not allowed to have my special freakin' day? Damn you! I deserve to at least live the full fairytale even if it doesn't last forever. All I want is one day where I am not reminded of my failed relationships. One day where I can feel like royalty. One day where I can pretend that I'm about to marry the perfect companion who only has eyes for me. One day that I can celebrate that love found me. *[Beat]* I have so much to give, so much to offer, and no one sticks. So here I am, with an open heart praying that there is a tiny chance that it will all work out.

It's my time. I waited long enough. So play along with me people. At least then I can say, "I did it, I had a glorious wedding. I was a beautiful bride for one fucking day." How hard is it to allow me to experience that? Huh? *(She slowly creeps over to a woman in the front row and claps her hands in her face.)*

Grandma, you wanna wake up? Did you ever to stop to think that maybe I threw my own wedding sooner rather than later so that you can be alive to witness it? *(She picks up her bouquet and hops back up on stage.)* I heard about this woman who killed her whole entire family because she was fed up…and here I am standing only three feet away from the cake cutter! So you all better shape up! You are going to pretend to have a fabulous time. You are going to laugh, cry and musicians, you're gonna get the music right because this isn't karaoke night in Vegas!

So let's start this again shall we? Everybody, start clapping. *(Scattered claps begin in the audience.)* Ok band, play! *(The Wedding March plays again. She calms herself down, and then re-adjusts her dress.)*

This is my damned day! My fairy tale! It's an experience that most women won't have in this lifetime, so don't screw it up!

(ELIZABETH places the veil back over her head and marches off-stage to the song.)

SELFIES

(Stagehands place a small coffee table and two chairs downstage. The music fades out. Lights up on GWEN, THE EX-FRIEND, seated with a teacup in hand. Gwen is a pretty English woman with short blond hair. Her scarf is tied into a bow around her belly. In front of her with her back to the audience is CORINNE, THE EXECUTIVE.)

GWEN

Is it too much to ask that you not text or take selfies while we are spending time together? I have a short lunch break and it's been a while since I've seen you. I mean I'm all for social media and self-promotion, but when you can't even acknowledge that I'm sitting directly in front of you at a lunch I'm paying for—then you're being rude.

I have to tell you, I simply cannot tolerate your selfish ways anymore. Frankly, I don't have time for it. To me a friendship is a two-way street. There can't always be one person giving while the other continues to take. It's draining, darling. It's obvious that you need that kind of companionship and I can no longer provide that for you. I came here to tell you that I'm pregnant and it's taken me this entire lunch hour to get you to put your damn phone down to hear my good news.

What is it with everyone and their damn phones? Yes at times it's convenient to be buried in your device, but not all day long— especially when you are out with friends. This addiction that society has with technology, to the extent that you can't even carry on a conversation without someone looking down to text, is pathetic. I'm worried about bringing a child into this world where people do not remember how to communicate with their God given voices.

And another thing, this obsession you have with posting constant updates on Facebook is annoying. Countless people sharing every detail about their day as if Facebook were their personal diary. It's simply not ladylike to obsess about the numbers of people commenting on what you say or how you look, all the time. Is this what builds one's self-belief these days? For heaven's sake stop prostituting yourself for positive "comments" and "likes."

It seems to me that one's status update has become more important than the value of true words spoken in person. Can we all just learn to connect with one another on a person-to-person basis? Although I love social media, it has cut people off from each other. So for now…I'm logging off. And today you are paying for my lunch.

(GWEN bolts off stage.)

EMAIL TO MY BOSS

(THE EXECUTIVE flips her chair around and faces the audience. She's a brunette that has on glasses and a business suit. Corinne is holding her red scarf in her hand and tucked inside is her cell phone.)

CORINNE

Well, I guess she told me. I feel bad, but I was preoccupied with my phone for a good reason. I just received an obnoxious email from one of my employees. Wanna hear it? *(She reads an email on her cell phone to the audience.)*

Dear Corinne,

Sadly, I have recognized (like most of us in this pathetic, small, smelly, cramped office) that you are an egotistical bitch, and I'm not putting up with it anymore.

It has dawned on me that I am none the wiser, healthier, or happier than the day I started working here almost two years ago.

Normally I would tolerate your crap in an effort to keep collecting my paychecks, but I'm no longer afraid of losing my job. My quality of life is way more important than working beside you. Besides, I refuse to kiss your ass like everyone else does. Frankly you're not the type of person I would associate with outside of this office.

You seem so threatened by other women here at work that I've witnessed you pit them against each other just so you could be happy watching them fight.. And, they put up with the drama because they feel they have nowhere else to go.

How sad that so many smart, amazing women stick with their job, their man, their weight, all because they are too afraid of doing something about it.

You turned me down for a promotion that I deserved and when I asked you why you said "Oh, it wouldn't be a good fit for you." Then you went ahead and hired someone from Craigslist without any experience, for the big boss instead. There was no good reason for you to do that when I was the obvious choice. Some manager you are! What you did was not nice. I'm a smart and gifted woman that deserves a better job with better pay.

Environments like this create an atmosphere where people don't grow much and I see a bigger place for myself in the world, so in the end I want to thank you. You made my decision to move on easier.

While you reapply your Chanel lip-gloss to your paper-thin lips in your office, your assistant Mary is out there struggling to make ends meet so she can raise her two children on the poor salary you refuse to increase, knowing that you can. That's what gets me, you can help someone else but don't, for no other reason than to control the situation.

I won't need to clean out my desk. I don't need anything from it. You can keep the coffee mug that says, "Number One Secretary." Give it to Mary.

Lookout Corinne, some day you may be the one being replaced. This little company may fall flat on its ass in a year or less, or it may grow exponentially. Either way, I quit.

Best Regards,
Your ex-secretary
Elsie McFarland

(CORINNE tucks the cell phone along with the scarf into her purse. She glares into the audience perplexed.)

CORINNE

I don't have paper-thin lips...do I?

(Lights out.)

DADDY'S LITTLE GIRL

(In darkness CORINNE leaves and the stagehands swap out the loveseat for a park bench. Lights up. JAQUIE, THE DAUGHTER, runs in panting carrying a small basket of apples tied together with a red scarf.)

JAQUIE

Hey Dad! Happy Father's Day! Sorry, I'm late. I would have gotten here sooner, but I knew no one would be around and I wanted to make sure I had your full attention for once. I have to clear a few things up with you that have been bothering me pretty much all of my life.

After so many years, there is one question that I never had a chance to ask you, and Dad I really want to know the answer. Why wasn't I your favorite child? I was perfect to you. I never raised my voice, and was never disrespectful. Yet you didn't communicate with me about anything like you did with my brothers.

Is it because I'm moody? If so, Mom is way moodier than I am, she just doesn't seem to be having a good day if she hasn't put you down at least once. Not to mention that Jerry and Jesse are brats that never listened to you. *(She sits on the bench and places her basket down.)*

Is it my cooking? Because frankly Dad, I'm always going to be a vegan. The fact that grandpa ate the family pet rooster was not funny, it was rude and wrong and I hope he goes to hell for it. I was bothered that you didn't stand up to him and even more upset that you laughed about it. I think it's horrible what they do to animals so that our fat asses here in the USA can go to all-you-can-eat buffets clueless as to what enters our body.

Did you know that over 80% of factory farm animals carry salmonella and other forms of harmful bacteria that cause untreatable diseases in humans? Believe it or not, most of the diseases people get are meat related. It's a fact. And we eat that! I am not trying to convert you. I am well aware that there are medical instances where people need to eat meat, but I'm not one of those people. To each his own, but when I come over to visit, don't be offended when I say for the 20th time in a row, "No thanks I don't eat meat."

Did you not choose me because I'm too honest? I can't change that. I learned it from you. I like to tell it like it is and I have always been punished for being that authentic. Why? Did you want me to become a liar? Do you think that solves problems?

Is it because I'm not interested in having kids? Why would I do that Dad? I actually want to enjoy my life. Not that kids aren't great, I'm sure they are. But I saw how you and Mom struggled with the three of us when we were little, and I don't recall you having any fun. Besides I don't want to get married. I like going on lots of dates because for me life is about exploration. The thought of being with one person forever doesn't seem realistic, or normal to me.

I'd like to think that my soul mate is God, plus it saves me endless nights of tears over what didn't work out. If God's my soul mate then no man or woman can ever disappoint me. I think that is a much healthier way to live. Don't you agree? If I have kids one day, great! But don't criticize me if I choose not to.

What is it about me that kept you away? I wish I knew, because I am pretty freaking great. I read in a book that, usually, a girl will fall into a pattern of relationships in direct proportion to her relationship with her father. Well Dad, we don't have a relationship. Shocker, I'm single.

Daddy, I'm sorry. I didn't mean to come over here and dump on you... I just never had a heart to heart with you when you were alive.

(She weeps. JAQUIE picks up her basket of apples then kneels to the floor as if she's facing a tombstone. She unties the red scarf from the basket and wipes the tears from her cheeks.)

These apples are for you because you were the apple of my eye. I wish I knew more things about you like, what were your dreams? Did you ever want to travel? If you could pick another name for me, what would it have been?

Maybe I'm your favorite because we're exactly alike dad. Hopefully you're somewhere out in heaven watching over us, and hopefully through me you can live your life again.

Who knows? Maybe I was your favorite because I'm your only girl, and secretly the apple of your eye.

(She smiles to herself.)

(Lights out.)

A MOTHER'S RIGHT TO FEED

(Lights up on MICHELLE center stage. Throughout the show she has kept her red scarf around her shoulders.)

MICHELLE

I'm a breastfeeding mom. My relatives have an old school mentality when it comes to health. They think giving your kid a shot of whiskey when they are sick is a great medicinal cure. They're also the type that will dunk a child into a tub full of ice when they have a fever. That being said, you'd think when it came to breastfeeding, my relatives would be more open-minded. But that doesn't seem to be the case for my family and their friends.

The fact is that a mother's breast milk is the best option for feeding her baby. The benefits alone outweigh the flack you'll receive from ignorant folks who haven't done their research.

When breastfeeding isn't an option for a mom, then that is when you are encouraged to feed your child, formula, or whole cows' milk. And I am well aware that when a child is weaning, for many this becomes the next stage. But why rush into that phase sooner than you need to if you can help it? I have met so many moms who love breastfeeding and then there are those that cut it off for the sake of vanity, thus robbing their child of what they need from them too soon.

Obviously I'm not saying that this applies to everyone, so don't hate on me. I understand there are cases where a mom has to go back to work too soon, or pumping doesn't work out, I get it. What I'm talking about are the few women out there who have an attitude that says, "Everything is better than what God gave us to feed our children with. So go ahead, inject me and stop my milk 'cause I'd rather look good." It's fucked up.

Look, it ain't easy. For the first four months, I cried and grit my teeth while feeding my baby boy. But I thank God I stuck with it because one morning I woke up and it no longer hurt. Then the bonding between us truly kicked in full force. It was the most beautiful time I had with my son, gazing into his eyes as he drank milk peacefully. I sat appreciating how amazing our God is that he/she created our bodies to not only make children, but to feed them as well.

It saddens me to think that the animals on our planet, like the cows, are robbed of this gentle loving experience when their young are taken away and starved, while they are then forced to continue to lactate, which is painful.

Anyway, I'm at this family gathering when I decide to tuck myself away in another room to nurse my 13-month-old son. I will admit that my son looks more like a grown 2 or 3-year-old toddler, but he is still just a baby. And he's incredibly healthy I might add. I walk out of the room and my Mom's friend says judgmentally, "Don't you think he's a little too old for that? My God, he has teeth give him regular milk already."

That week I had noticed my son start to wean. Because of this I had become a little saddened over the realization that my breastfeeding days were numbered. I turned to my mom's friend and just exploded with,

"Well aren't you the perfect picture of health? Wasn't your daughter hospitalized several times because of her diet? If I remember correctly, she had an allergic reaction to milk proteins, like so many other children. You wanna know why? BECAUSE WE AREN'T FUCKING COWS!"

"To make matters worse the milk you drink from cows, isn't even milk anymore once it's fully processed. It's infused with hormones, chemicals and even pus with a little bit of blood mixed in. Yum! Sorry, it's gross but true.

"At least when I give my baby milk from me, there's none of that. He's getting 100% milk that isn't from a factory farm or fridge. If he needs to go that route, there are better options, so back off. If I want to feed him until he's 5-years-old then that is my choice and none of your business."

"I see you are drinking milk now? Um, aren't you a little too old for that? My God you have teeth! Grown-ups don't need milk past infancy. Educate yourself."

I'll admit it was a little bold and in your face, but fuck it, if they could be "honest," so could I. My mother was so embarrassed and I felt bad myself. Not because I lost it, but because I reacted. People are going to think what they want and judge me regardless and if I was feeling solid that day, I would have just said, "Keep your opinions to yourself, I have a mother's right to feed for however long I choose." And in my clarity that would have been the end of it. They were just being ignorant that's all. Hopefully next time I won't react at all.

(Lights change. Michelle sits on the edge of the stage.)

I use to think that the word insecurity meant: to be secure from the inside out. If that were true then it would be a good thing. After all, the way you see your problem is only a perception right? So maybe if we saw things differently any negative feelings or situations we had would disappear. *(She removes her scarf.)*

Maybe the whole point of the fear and self-doubt is to remind us to see it for what it truly is, an excuse to hold us apart from our greatness. So now that you know what I learned... let's stop.

(Michelle drops her red scarf to the floor. Lights out.)

THE POET

(A red spotlight shines on two CONGA PLAYERS performing. When they finish their solo an announcer invites a performer to the stage.)

ANNOUNCER

Welcome to the poetry slam. Coming to the stage, is someone you all know and love. She is no stranger to owning her power. You last saw her on *Superhero Defjam,* and most recently she was seen on TV flying her invisible plane, show your love to our next poet. Wonder Woman!

(A stunning African American spoken word artist, dressed as Wonder Woman, takes the stage. She was not part of the group that stepped onstage at the beginning of the show. She is also the only one who does not have a scarf in hand.)

WONDER WOMAN

Thank you. For those of you who don't know me, I'm Wonder Woman and I'm fierce. I have lived many years of my life as two separate identities. But tonight I am free to be Wonder Woman, fully.

As I gracefully dodge bullets and make villains confess the truth with my magic lasso, most women spend time dodging penises and playing the victim. My relationships were bad.

(She recites the next line as if she performing poetry. The conga players drum along.)

You see, Superman was only super in bed,
And Aqua Man swam away,
Spiderman was creepy,
And the Joker got away.

(Conga players stop. She laughs in spite of herself.)

WONDER WOMAN

Tonight's piece is titled "Choices."

(Musicians play their congas to the rhythm of her poem.)

WONDER WOMAN

It's like I'm swimming in the ocean with no water. At times, I'm drowning in quicksand, with no sand.

"Be you shine through?" I say as I look in the mirror, 'Be honest and true,' I chant as I walk out the door.

First person, second person third person I see, there is something they are hiding; but I'm not hiding me.

Fourth encounter stirs up thought; a quiet girl walks past. Everything is all smiles, but I can see this girl is sad.

Why is she holding it all in causing cancer to her soul? That counterfeit manner can't hide the truth, I know.

Did you open up your mouth and speak your heart today? Maybe something said or done that hurt you, wasn't meant that way.

Yet you grinned, took it in and just plain walked away, not honoring your soul which you encounter every day.

Fifth encounter, phone rings from a "friend" who speaks his mind.

He spends more time talking never listening, wasting your precious time.

Try sharing your opinion with these ones, who stated theirs,

Nope, they aren't even listening cause their ego's always there.

True friendship is about giving and receiving, not about taking without giving.

Or giving and giving, only expecting to be taken for a fool.

*We all have rules to living life, what
your rules are may not be mine.*

*Just remember those emotions
are the ones that you decide.*

Don't blame that on each other or you will live a lie.

*What empower means to me is, to embrace our
power or inspire others to reach much higher,*

*than your circumstances or the pain
you may feel, whatever it means to
you, "to thine own self be true."*

*They say life is short, but it can feel long if you
are wearing a mask and don't feel so strong.*

*It cuts off your breath there is no circulation,
so rip that mask off and
you will have your revelation.*

This message is for my friends, family and the haters too, there's abundance for all and that includes you.

*So this time step up and let your
light shine, and when you do, you
will see that you are divine.*

*Speak your heart with no regrets. You
are a superhero so don't you forget.*

Some may call you a bitch, but I prefer Goddess, in touch with your graceful feminine energy will make you stronger, not powerless.

(The conga players drum again. The women in the cast gather together and re-emerge onto the stage, each carrying their red scarves in hand. At the climax of the drumming they all toss them into the audience.)

WONDER WOMAN

Thank you. Goodnight.

BLACKOUT

THE END

Acknowledgements

Let's be real, if I had a bunch of famous people to acknowledge for this book, it means I'm already famous. And I'm not. I'm just a regular artist here to share a couple of stories that uplifted me and hopefully will do the same for you. My name is Jonisha Rios, and I'm a Puerto Rican Latina from Connecticut. In Hebrew, the name translates to John is a woman and trust me, I'm all woman, with a full array of colorful emotions to match.

After some let downs and broken promises in the world of entertainment, I realized what was most important to me was that I continued to create my works of art. So it was time to take a step back and write a book where I got to express my Latina flavor without having too many people interfere with how I went about doing that. Although my writing style isn't for everyone, hopefully, it will put a smile on your face or inspire some thought in you.

Many years ago when I began this journey, I was feeling very much alone. Not sure where my life was headed or if I'd ever find the loving relationship I deserved. That was when the chronicles of Cassandra were born, and *The Curse of the Blue Vagina* was created. In this story I got to dive in and indulge in the life of Cassandra, a quirky character that had a dilemma of her own.

This compilation of my work was originally two solo-shows produced and performed as a healing theatrical series across the nation. These pieces are fictional works inspired by some true events but completely exaggerated, so any likeness to people or incidents related to me is coincidental. In other words, they're just stories folks, so take pleasure in reading them.

My passion for writing began with my first solo-show, "Nude in New York." Shortly after that, I wrote and performed "The Curse of the Blue Vagina" (at one time titled "The Curse of the Blue Panties"), before it became this book compilation. That show was then followed by a private ensemble performance of a collection of monologues for women I produced, originally titled "Empow-Her." And finally my most recent collection of short stories, about a girl named Annabelle who inherits her deceased dad's strip club, became a mini web-series that I wrote, shot, and directed called "Saved by the Pole," (nominated for an *Imagen Award*. Special thanks to Ed Martin and Leo Rodriguez for producing that series.)

The point I'm trying to make is, I have been busy... and to top it off, I got pregnant. Turning at least two of these stage plays into a book has been a long journey and I'm thrilled that it's finally done. This book represents the completion of my trilogy of projects about shedding the masks that hide our truest self, thus the reason why the theme of nudity in each, exists.

There are many people to thank as this journey finally comes to an end:

First and foremost, to my loving and supportive husband, Michael Baez. Through the ups and downs, you have not only been my best friend, you have also been my teacher, my rock and my biggest fan. I thank you for your love and patience with my countless creative endeavors. As I put the finishing touches on this book, I am a week away from my thirty-something birthday and although I had hoped to get this out there before the birth of my first child, he arrived May 25th. Nothing I created with my husband compares to our greatest creation and gift from God, the love of my life Iysaac-Brendon or "Izzy-B." With my new role as a Mother, I'm ready to make space for the new stories popping up in my life.

A very special thanks to my amazing and wonderful sister and "clean-up team" Jennifer Rios, Jessica Lopez, Elizabeth Lopez, and Amber Fisher-McKone, who combed through this book with me, helping me organize and reconstruct these plays into a book.

I'd like to thank my crazy ass parents, Milagros and Johnny Rios. Because you allowed me to express myself as a kid, this voice was born.

A special thank you also goes out to Raymond Fisher, for inspiring me to pursue my artistic path when I was a child. Thanks to David Bianculli for becoming a new member of my crazy family. Julia, David and Henry for flying back and forth from NYC to Cali to support these projects when they were staged on the west coast. Love to all of you.

A very special thanks to the following people, whose

immense contribution to my vision helped this book manifest. Because of your continued support and encouragement, it's here.

For Nude in New York:

To the original casts and crews of all of my theatrical shows from Connecticut, NYC, Florida, Puerto Rico, and Los Angeles. George Leon, Jesse & James Mojica, Gaby & Sara Moreno, Lloyd Rodriguez, Delon Martinez, Charles Rice-Gonzalez and Arthur Aviles at B.A.A.D theatre in the Bronx, Julia Baez-Bonilla, David Baez, Dolly J. Wilberding, Juliet Zacarias, Delece James, Tanya Alexander, Kenn Scott, Joseph Babineaux, Jennifer Nieman, and two of my favorite repeat show watchers, Tiffany Phillips & Wesley Goo. I'd also like to give a shout out to my loving friends Andrew Hamrick & Onahoua Rodriguez.

To a couple of my favorite theatrical homes; The Los Angeles Women's Theatre Company, B.A.A.D Bronx, The Whitefire Theatre, my family at La Tea Theatre in NYC, just to name a few. And last but not least a heartfelt thanks to my grandparents and aunt, "Titi" Benny, to whom this show was dedicated.

For The Curse of the Blue Vagina:

Same as above including Nadine Valazquez, Gloria Calderon-Kellett, Veronica Caicedo, and Linda Mendoza. Many of you not only supported and inspired me, but also sat and listened to countless theatrical workshops of these pieces before they made it into this book.

To my Mentors: Kelly Kinsella, David Arnold, Eddy Pomerantz, Linda Mendoza, Michael and countless others out there whom I have looked up to; I am filled with gratitude having each of you in my life sharing your words of love, encouragement and wisdom, throughout all of my productions on and off screen. THANK YOU, THANK YOU, THANK YOU!

To my manager Marilyn Atlas, and my wonderful agent and publisher Leticia Gomez- Thank you for believing in me.

Many thanks to my artists, Ed Mouzon, Gary Camp, Adam "Illus" Wallenta, Timothy Pryor (my book cover artist), Debbi Stocco (my book designer), music artists, cameo supporters, and anyone I may not have men-tioned who has genuinely believed in the messages of my pieces. I'd also like to thank The Bronx Council on the Arts for making it all possible by awarding me with my first award for, Nude In NY! The money I won from that award launched my show. Thank you so much.

To my Grandparents and my Titi Witi:

I will always love you. Thank you for your inspiration. This cup of coffee is for you.

About the Author

Jonisha Rios attended University of Connecticut School of Fine Arts on dramatic scholarship and is a graduate of the American Musical and Dramatic Academy. She has studied at many different schools over the years fine-tuning her craft, including Second City, The Upright Citizens Brigade, and the Writers Guild of America East Screenwriting Workshop. Her projects include her star-studded web-series Saved by the Pole, Lionsgate world-wide distributed film A Wonderful Christmas-Feliz Navidad, award-winning short films Racket and Sweet Tooth. She's produced, co-created and directed commercials as well as several theatre productions including "Cursed. My road to Hollywood," with Linda Mendoza, and "I Never Met a Jerk I Didn't Like" by Tiffany Phillips.

Jonisha was one of the creators and head writers of a cable TV comedy sketch series "Unacceptable Behavior."

Her critically acclaimed solo show "Nude in New York" garnered her attention and numerous awards including a BRIO award for Outstanding Achievement in the arts. Her second solo show "The Curse of the Blue Panties" was the inspiration for this book. All theatrical pieces have been performed on east and west coast stages.

Jonisha currently teaches solo-show and creative writing workshops at colleges and children's after school programs. She has also coached celebrities, fellow actors and even kids one-on-one wanting to create their own theatrical pieces. To hire her for your next event check out, www.blameitonrioslive.com for more info.

Finally, Jonisha is co-creator of the "Awakened Warrior" 200 & 500 hour yoga teacher-training program nationwide led by Michael Baez. If you have any interest in becoming a yoga teacher visit, www.AWYTT.com

And when she isn't teaching or practicing yoga, she is at home snuggled up, breastfeeding and spending quality time enjoying every moment with her precious son Iysaac-Brendon.

www.ingramcontent.com/pod-product-compliance
Lightning Source LLC
Chambersburg PA
CBHW020402080526
44584CB00014B/1143